THEMATIC UNIT

Rivers and Ponds

Written by Jeanne King and Ellen Krogman

Teacher Created Materials, Inc.
P.O. Box 1040
Huntington Beach, CA 92647
©1997 Teacher Created Materials, Inc.
Made in U.S.A.

ISBN-1-57690-114-9

Illustrated by
Phil Hopkins

Edited by
Charlene Stout

Cover Art by
Sue Fullam & José Tapia

Table of Contents

Introduction

Rivers and Ponds is a captivating whole language thematic unit. It contains 80 exciting pages filled with a wide variety of lesson ideas and activities designed for use with primary children. At its core are four high-quality children's literature selections, *All Eyes on the Pond*, *Frog and Toad Together*, *Look Closer: Pond Life* and *Look Closer: River Life*. For each of these books, activities are included which set the stage for reading, encourage the enjoyment of the book, and extend the concepts gained. In addition, the theme is connected to the curriculum with activities in language arts, math, science, social studies, art, cooking, and physical education. Many of these activities encourage cooperative learning. Suggestions for a bulletin board, a research center, and unit management are additional timesavers for busy teachers. Directions for big books, a poetry unit, and a culminating activity will allow students to synthesize and share their knowledge beyond the classroom. Altogether, these activities comprise a very complete teacher resource on pond and river life.

This thematic unit includes the following:

❑ **planning guides**—suggestions for sequencing lessons each day of the unit

❑ **literature selections**—summaries of four children's books with related lessons and activities (complete with reproducible pages) that cross the curriculum

❑ **poetry**—suggested selections and lessons that enable students to write and publish their own works

❑ **group projects**—activites to foster cooperative learning

❑ **planning guides**—suggestions for sequencing lessons each day of the unit

❑ **writing and language experience ideas**—daily suggestions for writing activities across the curriculum, including big books, minibooks, pop-up book, poetry books, and journals

❑ **bulletin board ideas**—suggestions and plans for student-created interactive bulletin boards

❑ **curriculum connections**—activities and lesson in language arts, math, science, social studies, art, physical education, and cooking

❑ **a culminating activity**—ideas which require students to synthesize their learning to produce a product or engage in an activity that can be shared with others

❑ **a bibliography**—suggested additional literature including nonfiction books, educational magazines, and software related to the theme

---

> To keep this valuable resource intact so that it can be used year after year, you may wish to punch holes in the pages and store them in a three-ring binder.

Introduction _(cont.)_

Why Balance Basic Skills and Whole Language?

The strength of a whole language approach is that it involves children in using all modes of communication—reading, writing, listening, illustrating, and interacting. Communication skills are interconnected and integrated into lessons that emphasize the whole of language. Balancing this approach is our knowledge that every whole—including individual words—is composed of parts, and directed study of those parts can help a student to master the whole. Experience and research tell us that regular attention to phonics, word attack skills, spelling, etc., develops reading mastery, thereby completing the unity of the whole language experience. The child is thus led to read, write, spell, speak, and listen confidently in response to a literature experience introduced by the teacher. In these ways, language skills grow rapidly, stimulated by direct practice, active involvement, and interest in the topic at hand.

Why Thematic Planning?

A whole language program is best implemented with thematic planning. The teacher plans classroom activities correlated to specific literature selections centered around a predetermined theme. Students tend to learn and retain more when they are applying their skills in an interesting and meaningful context. Both teachers and students will be freed from a day that is broken into unrelated segments of isolated drill and practice.

Why Cooperative Learning?

Students need to learn social appropriateness as well as academic skills. This area of development can not be taken for granted. Because group activities are a part of living, it is important to consider social objectives in your planning. Students working together will select leaders and designate responsibilities within their groups. The teacher is present to explain social goals and monitor interaction.

Why Make Big Books?

An excellent cooperative, whole language activity is the production of Big Books. Groups of students, or the whole class, can apply their language skills, content knowledge, and creativity to produce a Big Book that can become a part of the classroom library to be read and reread. These books make excellent culminating projects for sharing beyond the classroom with parents, librarians, and other classes. This unit contains specific directions for three of the many methods to produce Big Books.

Why Journals?

Each day your students should have the opportunity to write in a journal. They may respond to a book or an historic event, write about a personal experience, or answer a general question of the day posed by the teacher. The cumulative journal provides an excellent means of documenting writing progress.

Why Learning Centers?

A learning center is a special area of the classroom set aside for the study of a specific topic, creation of a related project, completion of an experiment, or expression of an idea through a fine arts activity.

All Eyes on the Pond
by Michael J. Rosen

The creatures that inhabit the pond gaze, walk, swoop, whoosh, peer, jump, paddle, skitter, and much more as the book invites the reader to view the pond through the day and into the night, discovering a world rarely seen. The eerie sense of watchfulness beckons the reader into the quiet world of the pond to see what the pond sees. The vivid imagery of Rosen's simple verse, along with Tom Leonard's enchanting illustrations, captivates the young reader's imagination with a close-up of each animal and its small world.

The outline below is a suggested plan for using the activities presented in the unit. You may adapt these ideas to fit your own classroom situation.

Sample Plan

Lesson 1

- Create a chart of pond animals and sounds. (page 6)
- Complete What Is a Pond? (page 8)
- Begin Journal Topics. (page 42)
- Imitate sounds of the pond to create a classroom pond symphony. (page 6)
- Do the Pond Dipping project. (page 10)
- Read and answer questions about pond life. (page 9)

Lesson 2

- Read *All Eyes on the Pond*.
- Continue Journal Topics. (page 42)
- Construct classroom ponds. (page 64)
- Create All Eyes on the Rivers and Ponds pocket folders. (page 6)
- Introduce Pond Animals and Pond Plants. (pages 11 and 12)
- Plan a trip to a local pond to observe the plant and animal life firsthand.

Lesson 3

- Complete the Meet More Pond Animals cut and paste activity. (pages 14 and 15)
- Introduce the bulletin board and research center. (pages 6 and 7)
- Complete Leap Frog Math. (page 57)
- Illustrate an animal of the pond to add to the bulletin board.
- Introduce Busy Beavers. (page 13)

Lesson 4

- Begin Seasons of the Pond activity. (pages 59 and 60)
- Construct Underwater Pond Scope. (page 63)
- Complete Lily Pad Compounds. (page 45)
- Do Problems to "Pond"er. (page 53)

Lesson 5

- Continue Journal Topics.
- Complete Seasons of the Pond activity. (pages 59 and 60)
- Complete the Don't Break the Surface! experiment. (page 16)
- Begin graphing activities. (page 54)
- Prepare recipes from Pond Food Festival. (pages 74 and 75)
- Write river and pond poetry. (pages 49 and 50)

Overview of Activities

Setting the Stage

1. Show the class the book *All Eyes on the Pond*. Explain that when they visit a pond, they will see a variety of different plants and animals. Create a chart of some of the animals students think they might meet at the pond. Include a column to write the sounds the students think the animals might make.

2. Play a recording of environmental sounds that showcase the pond. Have students listen quietly for a few moments with their eyes closed. What kinds of animals do they visualize? Add these animal names and sounds to the chart.

3. Create a classroom pond symphony. Ask students to choose one of the animals of the pond and imitate the sound that animal makes. Begin with the sound of one student and add more sounds of the pond, one at a time, until the entire classroom is filled with this wildlife chorus.

4. Complete the What Is a Pond? activity on page 8.

5. Begin a Rivers and Ponds bulletin board with the research center (Enjoying the Book, #9). Set up the background for the students. Be sure to include old tree trunks and spaces for those animals that live around the pond. Label library pocket cards and staple them next to the plant or animal picture. As children create the various art and language activities in this unit, include these on your bulletin board.

6. Sing "Over in the Meadow." Use it as a pattern to create a class song about pond and river life.

Enjoying the Book

1. Read *All Eyes on the Pond*, pointing out the closeup of each animal on each page of the book.

2. Ask students to graph their favorite pond animal from graphing activities on page 54. Remember to build from the bottom up with student picture squares.

3. Begin the Pond and River Watchers' Diary, using the handout on page 32. Each day of your study, showcase one animal of the pond from the Meet More Pond Animals handouts on pages 14 and 15, or the *Look Closer: Pond Life* book. Before writing, use guided imagery to not only help the children visualize what the animal looks like but also imagine other sights and sounds they can imagine occurring at the pond each day. Brainstorm the students' responses on the board before each writing session.

4. Have students create All Eyes on the Rivers and Ponds pocket folders to keep their work in. Students will each need two pieces of 12" x 18" (30 cm x 45 cm) construction paper. **Fold** the first paper in half (hamburger fold). **Fold** the second paper in half lengthwise (hot dog fold) and then **fold** the second paper in half once again (hamburger fold). **Staple or tape** the second paper into the bottom half of the first paper. You have a pocket folder ideal for keeping completed work on the inside and work in progress in the outside pockets. These can be titled and decorated creatively to go in their portfolios.

Overview of Activities *(cont.)*

Enjoying the Book *(cont.)*

5. Read and guide students through Meet More Pond Animals (pages 14 and 15). Do the cut and paste activity.

6. Review your animal sounds chart. Have the students write original poetry (pages 49 and 50).

7. Do the Problems to "Pond"er word problems on page 53.

8. Have students learn about pond life by completing the activities on page 9–13.

9. Complete the Pond Map on page 58. For younger students this will be a good listening activity while older students may be able to read the directions on their own. You also might wish to introduce students to the compass rose. (Remember the directional mnemonic "Never Eat Soggy Waffles.")

10. Set up your research center with appropriate books, magazines, index cards, writing materials, crayons, markers, and colored pens or pencils. Have each student choose a pond animal to research, illustrate, paint, and cut out for the pond bulletin board. They can use index cards to write one to two things about a plant or animal displayed on the board. The index cards are then placed in the library pocket cards on the bulletin board. Thus, students study about the pond and river from the bulletin board.

Extending the Book

1. Complete the Seasons of the Pond activity on pages 59 and 60. Discuss the different changes and which animals might be most affected by seasonal changes.

2. Use the poetry ideas on pages 49 and 50 to make standing poetry books. These are wonderful keepers for open house, portfolios, or parent conferences. After students have written their poems, have them copy the poems onto 3" x 5" (8 cm x 13 cm) index cards. Next, take a piece of large construction paper and fold it lengthwise. Fold the paper into thirds and fan-fold the paper to make a free-standing display. Have the students paste up to six cards on their displays. Students then illustrate around the cards with pictures from the river and/or pond.

3. Create frog and snail ponds in the classroom, using the materials and directions on page 64.

4. Set up an aquarium in the classroom with either small fish, turtles, or even small frogs. A sample pond aquarium diagram is provided on page 10. You'll need to set things up differently for each animal, so check with your local pet store about a good mix of animals.

5. Have students collect, measure, and mount items they might find in the pond. These can be plastic or ceramic animals, leaves, twigs, or even blades of grass.

6. The water strider is a fascinating pond insect. Students will discover why it can walk on water with the activity on page 16.

7. Enjoy some of the Pond Food Festival treats on pages 74 and 75.

What Is a Pond?

A pond is a small, shallow body of water surrounded by land. These mini-lakes are found on farms, in parks, backyards, and out in the wild. Many animals and plants grow in and around the pond. A layer of clay or rock under the pond's muddy bottom keeps the water from soaking down into the ground. These shallow ponds allow the sun's light energy to reach down where water plants grow and provide food for many of the small pond animals.

After reading the information above, add your own plants and animals to the picture. Color the picture.

Complete the following activities on the back of this paper.

1. Name six water plants.

2. Name ten small animals that live in and around the pond.

Pond Life

Ponds are homes to many kinds of animals and plants. Most small ponds are formed when rainwater fills small holes in the ground, but most of these soon dry up. Some people make ponds in parks or on farms or even in backyards. All of the ponds that do not dry up are called **permanent ponds**.

Permanent ponds have a layer of clay or rock under their muddy bottoms that keeps the water from soaking away. The water is usually shallow, which lets sunlight reach the bottom. Sunlight gives plants the energy they need to make their food and helps the pond plants grow. These plants provide food for many of the small pond animals. If a pond rests in the shade, there will be less wildlife, so look for ponds in open areas when you want to explore.

In many ponds, you may find many different grasses, wildflowers, like the marsh marigold, and trees, such as willows and alders. You have to look closely to find tiny water plants called algae covering the mud of the pond or growing in clumps that look like sheep's wool. Some water weeds, like duckweed and water fern, float on the surface of the water. Pond weed and water milfoil grow completely under water, and water crowfoot, snakeweed, and arrowhead have some leaves above and some below the surface.

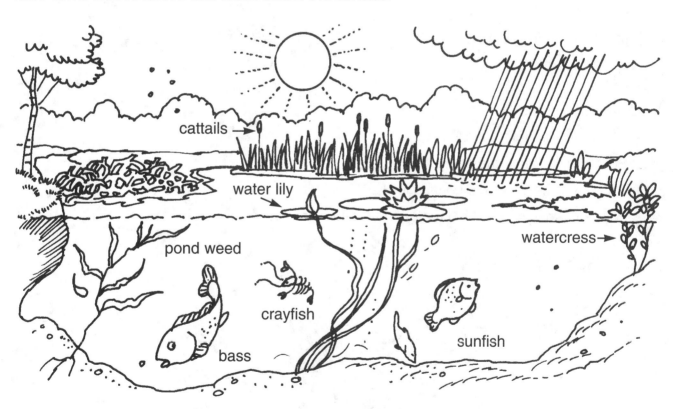

After reading the information, add your own pond animals to the picture.

Complete the following activities on the back of this paper.

1. Name three plants you might find in a pond.

2. Why are plants important to the pond?

Pond Dipping

Pond dipping allows you to study many of the tiny critters that live in puddles, ponds, streams, and ditches. Some breathe under the water through gills. Others must come up for air. But all will need water to survive!

Since hand dipping harms these animals, you'll need a large collection jar to scoop up some of their water. With a soft net, you just dip and turn it inside out into the jar so the critters swim off unharmed. Before going pond dipping, you'll need to plan ahead and gather up a few items.

Materials

- large clear plastic jar or tub
- foot end of an old stocking
- needle and thread
- 2 feet (.72 m) of wire and tape
- bamboo pole
- small magnifying glass
- small aquarium

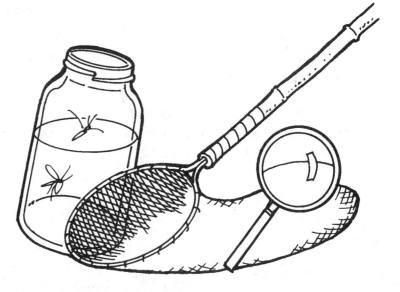

Directions

- Bend the wire into a circle.
- Push the wire into the end of the pole.
- Tape over the wire/pole connection.
- Fold and sew the stocking material over the wire circle.

Diagram of Pond Aquarium

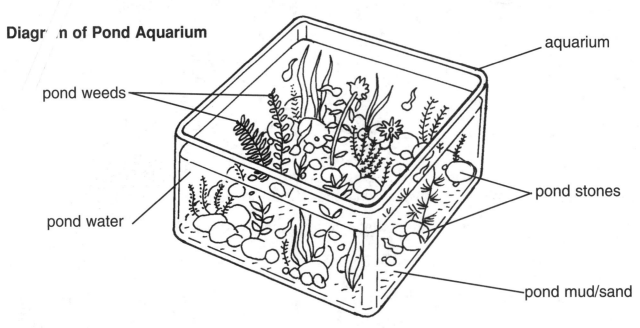

aquarium

pond weeds

pond stones

pond water

pond mud/sand

Pond Animals

In the miniature world of ponds and rivers, tiny animals are both the hunters and the hunted. Take this sheet to a small pond and check each tiny animal you observe. On the back, write down anything else you learned about pond life.

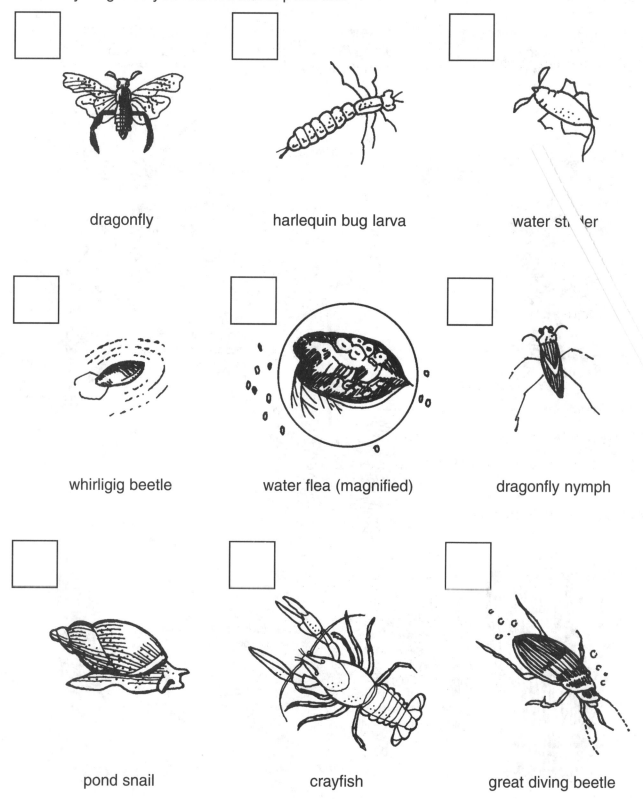

dragonfly

harlequin bug larva

water strider

whirligig beetle

water flea (magnified)

dragonfly nymph

pond snail

crayfish

great diving beetle

Pond Plants

Some plants need watery homes to survive. The water lily cannot live on dry land. We are charmed by its sweet-smelling flowers floating on broad lily pads. Few of us bother to look under the leaf to discover its long hollow stalks leading down into the depths. In the sandy mud at the bottom of ponds and rivers we find the water lily's roots anchored deep, holding the plant in its most favorite spot. Air pockets enable these leaves to support frogs sitting topside while water snails crawl slowly along their undersides. The giant Amazon water lily is so large that a small person could stand on it without sinking.

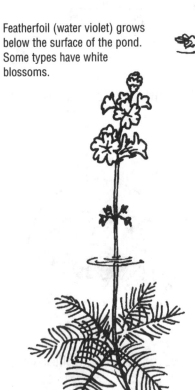

Featherfoil (water violet) grows below the surface of the pond. Some types have white blossoms.

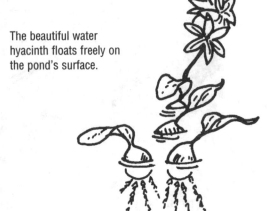

Water crowfoot has two kinds of leaves, wide "floaters" on the water and feathery leaves below.

Milfoil's long leaves look much like land plants. But they grow under the water.

Cattails grow at the edges of ponds and streams. Their strong, tall stems rise above the water level to provide homes for nesting animals. At the top, flowering spikes of brown velvet burst open to reveal a soft, cottony fluff and seedy nuts.

The beautiful water hyacinth floats freely on the pond's surface.

12

Busy Beavers

Beavers affect the land and the lives of other wildlife more than any other wild animal. With only branches, sticks, and mud, these industrious rodents build large dams that can flood hundreds of acres of land. The trees and smaller flooded plants die. The natural homes of many other animals are destroyed and washed away by the rampaging flood waters. When the waters subside, nature gradually returns to normal but to a different landscape. Results of the beavers' work has often created new and sometimes large wetland areas. Fish swim back upstream to prosper in small beaver ponds. Water birds and larger animals return to browse the shallow waters of lakes and rivers. Plants again flourish along the muddy shores. The beaver is truly the master architect of the animal world.

This cutaway view shows the beavers' log dam, their lodge, and their stockpile of food for the winter.

Beavers artfully pile branches and sticks to make their lodge, often six feet across. A mud "plaster" fills in the spaces, freezes in the winter, and a solid wall soon blocks the river. At the top of the lodge, a loose pile of branches rises several feet out of the water. This is to allow air to enter the lodge living area.

Nearby, branches are anchored in the pond mud. To get food in winter, beavers follow underwater tunnels that lead from the dam into the living chamber and out the back to the food storage area.

Meet More Pond Animals

1. Read to learn more about some animals you will find in many ponds.

2. Color, cut, and paste each animal in the box next to its description.

I am a **frog**! I began my life in the water as a tadpole, and as I grew larger, my tail shrank, I grew arms and legs, and I developed lungs. My large eyes on the top of my head are very sensitive to movement. I have a long, sticky tongue that darts out quickly to catch those tasty insects, slugs, and snails I love to eat.

I am a **newt**, one of the shy relatives of the frog. I began my life as a tadpole also. Once I developed into an adult newt, I went to live on land for part of the year. Most of the time I hide out of sight under moist leaves or rocks, and I come out at night to feed on worms, slugs, insects, or snails. In winter, I go to sleep or hibernate under rocks or in cracks or in the bark of dead trees. In spring, I return to the pond to mate and lay eggs.

I am the **dragonfly**. I hover over the pond using my large, powerful wings to fly backwards and forwards in search of food. I hunt for water insects and small fish, which I usually eat while flying. My giant, bulging eyes cover most of my head, and each eye has over 30,000 sides called lenses. My lenses see moving things up to 60 feet (18 m) away.

I am a **pond snail**, and I breathe underwater through my skin. I move slowly up and down the water plants, using my large, flat foot as I search for food. I have a special hole in my body so I can take in air from the pond's surface. My hard shell protects me from danger and grows as I grow.

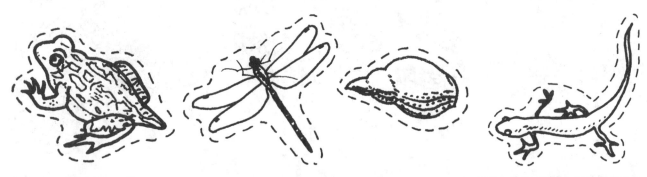

Meet More Pond Animals *(cont.)*

1. Read to learn more about some animals you will find in many ponds.

2. Color, cut, and paste each animal in the box next to its description.

I am a **duck**! I am one of many birds called waterfowl that may spend part of the year at the pond. I have webbed feet for swimming and a flexible neck well suited for grabbing things in the water. My feathers are covered with a protective coating that keeps water from coming in close contact with my skin, so I don't get cold in the water. The water beads and shakes off me easily.

Shhh! I am the **water strider**! I live on the surface of quiet waters and prey on other insects. Each pair of my six legs has a very specific purpose. My front two legs are adapted for grasping my prey. I use my middle pair of legs as paddles for moving across the water, and I use my hind legs for steering. Fine, dense hairs on my feet keep me from breaking the surface film of the water, so I don't sink.

I am a **turtle**! I eat just about anything, from small water animals to parts of trees to animal remains. I have webbed or flipper-like feet that help me swim in the water and a leather skin covering on my underside, which helps me absorb oxygen.

We are the **jelly babies**! You'll see us floating by the shores of the pond in spring. We are clumps of frog eggs (some people call us **frogspawn**) covered with a protective jelly-like coating that helps protect us from molds, bacteria, or microscopic creatures. At first, we sink to the bottom of the pond. Our jelly covering soon swells with water, and we float to the surface. About two weeks later, we hatch into tiny tadpoles.

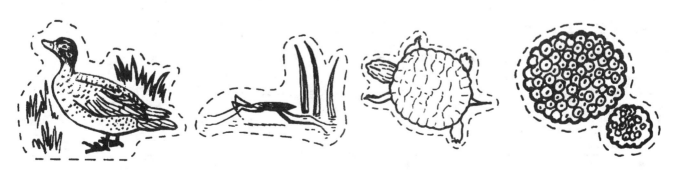

Don't Break the Surface!

Have you ever seen a water strider walk on water or watched a leaf floating on the surface of a puddle? Why don't they sink? It's simple—surface tension!

Water molecules have the amazing ability to bind or stick together, creating an invisible skin on the surface of the water. Many animals and plants use this invisible skin when they float. Ducks and water lilies float; yet, if pushed underwater, they will sink. Some insects, like the water strider, can actually walk across this invisible skin. Whenever you see a water droplet or bead of water, you are really looking at many water molecules that are sticking together and creating an invisible skin.

Activity

Work with a partner (and an eyedropper) on the experiment below to find the material that water beads up on. Then record the information on the worksheet.

What do I want to learn from this activity? _____

_____

Material	Soaks In (absorbs)	Beads Up
1. cloth		
2. paper towel		
3. wax paper		
4. plastic wrap		
5. glass or metal		

What materials did the water bead up on? _____

_____

Which materials would you use to make rain gear out of? Why?_____

_____

What did I learn from this activity? _____

_____

Frog and Toad Together

by Arnold Lobel

Summary

Frog and Toad Together *details the adventures of Frog and Toad in five lively, readable short stories. Students will enjoy reading these tales of Frog and Toad's friendship, starting with "A List" and "The Garden" through the stories about "Cookies" and "Dragons and Giants," and finishing with "The Dream." In "A List," Toad makes a list of all the things he must do in his day, only to lose his list halfway through his day. The story "The Garden" tells of Frog's wish to create his very own garden, just like Toad's, but he needs help in getting his seeds to grow, after a few comically unsuccessful attempts. In "The Cookies" the friends work hard to keep from eating all of Toad's freshly baked cookies. The final two stories, "Dragons and Giants" and "The Dream," focus on themes of bravery and loneliness.*

The outline below is a suggested plan for using the various activities that are presented in this unit. You may adapt these ideas to fit your own classroom situations.

Sample Plan

Lesson 1

- Create a chart of Frog Facts.
- Do the Froggy Facts and Opinions handout. (page 23)
- Introduce additional books to the research center.
- Learn Facts About Amphibians. (page 22)
- Play Leapfrog.

Lesson 2

- Read "A List."
- Use the Journal Topics. (page 42)
- Do the What Time Is It? worksheet. (page 25)
- Complete the Amphibian Life Cycle. (page 26)
- Do an art activity. (pages 67–72)
- Try Pond Food Festival recipes. (pages 74 and 75)

Lesson 3

- Read "The Garden."
- Do How Does Your Garden Grow? (page 27)
- Continue graphing activities. (page 54)

Lesson 4

- Read "Cookies."
- Complete the Cooperative Cookie Math activity. (pages 55 and 56)
- Write a Recipe for a Perfect Friendship. (page 28)
- Complete the When Is a Frog Not a Frog? Venn diagram. (page 61)
- Complete Pond Directions. (page 58)
- Write letters about pond or river life. (page 46)
- Introduce The Pond Readers' Theater and assign parts. (pages 20 and 21)

Lesson 5

- Read "Dragons and Giants."
- Write a sequel using Mini-Book form on page 24.
- Play frog games. (page 73)
- Complete the Friends: Are You More Alike or Different? Venn diagram. (page 62)
- Brainstorm words and phrases about tadpoles growing into frogs.
- Perform the Readers' Theater.

Overview of Activities

Setting the Stage

1. Have the students sit in a circle and pass a small sponge or rubber ball from one child to the next. When the teacher says "Frog" the student holding the ball has to say one thing he or she knows about a frog. After students have heard all the responses, create a KWL chart, representing three categories (what I already **know**, what I **want to learn**, and what I **learned**). In the first column of the chart (K—what I know) record the students' responses from the activity above. Display the chart and add student responses to the remaining two columns as the unit progresses. Discuss the KWL chart information at the end of this section. Extension: Complete a KWL chart about rivers and ponds, to be completed at the end of the unit.

2. Discuss the difference between a fact and an opinion. A fact is something that is always true and an opinion is something that might change depending on who says it (Fact: "A frog is an amphibian." Opinion: "A frog is cute."). Together, complete the Froggy Facts and Opinions activity on page 23. Have the students write F for fact and O for Opinion next to each response.

3. Encourage each student to learn about amphibians with Facts About Amphibians (page 22). Cut the boxes to make information cards. If possible, laminate them for durability. Encourage students to each learn a new fact a day. Use a chart or other recording device to indicate the students' progress as they learn the facts on the cards.

4. Extend your research center to include frog books, such as *The Complete Frog: A Guide for the Very Young Naturalist* and the *Audubon Guide to Reptiles and Amphibians*.

5. Start a classroom frog collection. Encourage children to bring in stuffed, ceramic, or plastic frogs or toads from home to display on their desks or in a special area of the classroom during the study of *Frog and Toad Together*.

Enjoying the Book

1. Begin reading *Frog and Toad Together* with the story, "A List." Have students make their own lists of what they do each day. After students finish, ask them to write the time of day they usually complete each task. For younger children, create a simplified class list and put the times beside the tasks.

2. Complete the What Time Is It? worksheet on page 25. In the last box, students write an activity on the lines and draw the hands.

3. Using the information and life cycle diagram on page 26, discuss the life cycle of the amphibian with the class. Have students complete the activity at the bottom of the page to show the life cycle of a frog.

4. Read "The Garden" from *Frog and Toad Together*. In this chapter, Toad reads, sings songs, and plays music in order to make his plants grow. Have the students measure each plant's growth, using How Does Your Garden Grow? (page 27)

Overview of Activities *(cont.)*

Enjoying the Book *(cont.)*

5. Reproduce the Readers' Theater script on pages 20 and 21. Assign roles and encourage students to practice their parts whenever possible. Students can make simple props and costumes and perform the readers' theater for the class, or other classes when they finish this section of the unit.

6. Read "The Cookies" from *Frog and Toad Together*. Bring in copies of recipes for students to look over. Point out the ingredients list, directions for putting things together, and the listing for time and temperature. Have students create "Recipe for a Perfect Friendship." (page 28)

7. Read "Dragons and Giants." Discuss how Frog and Toad were brave together as they climbed the mountain and faced their fears. They were grateful to have each other as friends. Ask students to think about Frog and Toad's adventures throughout the book. Have them think about how Frog and Toad alike and how they are different. Distribute the Venn diagram on page 62 and have students work in pairs to complete the activity.

8. Choose from the froggy journal topics on page 42. Have students write on a regular basis throughout the unit. When the unit is complete, ask students to break into small groups to role play, or otherwise share, their journal entries.

Extending the Book

1. Do the Cooperative Cookies math activities from pages 55 and 56. Create a cover. Bind the pages into a book for your classroom library.

2. Set up an Arnold Lobel center featuring all the *Frog and Toad* books along with other books by the author. Give awards to any students who read five or more of Lobel's books within a given time.

3. Have students complete some or all of the following art activities: frog puppet (page 67), paper plate frog (page 68), tissue paper polliwog (page 68), 3-D lily pad (page 69). The projects can used for bulletin board displays, prompts for writing and poetry activities, or as theme displays around the room.

4. Write a cartoon strip to create a sequel to *Frog and Toad Together* using the mini-book on page 24.

5. Set up a letter writing center, so students can write to friends. Use the letter-writing form on page 46. Have students decorate paper bags to hang on their chairs, so each student will have their own mailbox. Place stickers to be used as stamps, along with extra pencils, envelopes, and paper at the center.

6. Play the "Frogs and Flies" and "Frog in the Pond" activities on page 73.

7. As a culmination activity for *Frog and Toad Together*, have students share their completed work by telling what they learned about frogs, toads, friendship, etc.

8. Enjoy some of the Pond Food Festival treats on pages 74 and 75.

The Pond Readers' Theater

Narrator 1: Newt and Salamander lived on the bank of a pond. They loved to play together. One day they watched a beautiful dragonfly flying overhead.

Newt: Look how high Dragonfly can fly. I wish I could fly!

Salamander: Maybe Dragonfly will teach us, Newt.

Newt: Let's ask!

Newt and Salamander: How do you fly, Dragonfly?

Dragonfly: That's easy! I just close my eyes and float on the breeze.

Narrator 2: So Newt and Salamander stood on the bank of the pond and closed their eyes. But nothing happened.

Newt: Did you fly, Salamander?

Salamander: No, did you, Newt?

Newt: I don't think so. Maybe we need to jump first.

Narrator 3: Newt and Salamander held hands and jumped as high as they could into the air.

Narrator 4: Splash! Newt and Salamander fell into the pond.

Salamander: I guess we can't fly, Newt. Let's go and watch the ducks.

Narrator 1: Newt and Salamander wandered over to the other side of the pond where Duck floated by on the surface of the water.

Newt: Look at how easily Duck can float, Salamander. I wish I could float.

Salamander: Maybe Duck will show us, Newt.

Newt: Let's ask!

Newt and Salamander: How do you float, Duck?

Duck: That's easy! I just close my eyes and rest on the water.

The Pond Readers' Theater *(cont.)*

Narrator 2:   Newt and Salamander stood on the bank of the pond and closed their eyes. But nothing happened.

Newt: Did you float, Salamander?

Salamander: No, did you, Newt?

Newt: I don't think so. Maybe we need to jump first.

Narrator 3:   Newt and Salamander held hands and jumped high into the air.

Narrator 4:   Splash! Newt and Salamander fell into the pond.

Salamander: I guess we can't float, Newt. Let's go watch the frogs.

Narrator 1:   Newt and Salamander wandered over to the lily pads where Frog hopped from flower to flower.

Newt: Look how far Frog hops, Salamander. I wish I could hop.

Salamander: Maybe Frog will teach us, Newt.

Newt: Let's ask!

Newt and Salamander: How do you hop, Frog?

Frog: That's easy! I just close my eyes and hop from lily to lily.

Narrator 2:   Newt and Salamander closed their eyes and stood on the bank of the pond. But nothing happened.

Newt: Did you hop, Salamander?

Salamander: No, did you, Newt?

Newt: I don't think so. Maybe we need to jump first.

Narrator 3:   Newt and Salamander held hands and jumped high into the air.

Narrator 4:   Splash! Newt and Salamander fell into the pond.

Salamander: I guess we can't hop, Newt. What do we do?

Newt: I don't know, Salamander. Let's think about it.

Narrator 1:   Newt and Salamander thought about it as they crawled home.

Facts About Amphibians

Amphibians are fascinating creatures that lead double lives. After they hatch from their eggs, they live underwater until their gills disappear and their lungs develop. Then they hop or crawl out of the water and begin a new life on land. No amphibians live in the ocean.

Amphibians are divided into three groups: those with tails such as newts and salamanders, those without tails such as frogs and toads, and those without feet such as caecilians.

All toads are frogs, but all frogs are not toads. Toads are usually bumpier than frogs and live on land. Frogs have smoother skin and live around water. If you happen to see a frog or a toad, just refer to it as a frog and you'll always be right.

Male frogs often have sacs under their chins that look like bubbles when puffed up. These sacs help make the frogs' voices louder when they sing. Some frogs use one "bubble" to sing, while others use double bubbles to sing.

Relatives of the frog were among the first animals to live on land. Before dinosaurs lumbered along, frog relatives were leaping everywhere. Worldwide, there are now over 3,000 varieties of frogs.

Amphibians drink water differently than people do. Instead of taking water in through their mouths, they drink water in through their skin. Amphibians also lose water through their skin so they always have to stay in damp places. If they don't they will dry out and die.

When the ponds freeze over in winter, some amphibians bury themselves in the soft mud on the bottom and hibernate through the winter. Since these animals are sleeping, their bodies get cold and almost stop working. They hardly need any oxygen. They absorb the oxygen they do need in through their skin from the ooey-gooey mud.

Our body temperature stays pretty much the same. An amphibian's body temperature changes along with the air temperature around it. If a frog or a salamander gets too hot on a summer day, it has to find a moist and shady place where it can cool off. On a very cool day, the amphibian needs to find a sunny spot where it can warm its muscles; otherwise, it will have difficulty moving.

Froggy Facts and Opinions

A fact is a true statement that can be looked up in an encyclopedia or other scientific book. An opinion is a statement that tells what somebody believes or how they feel about something. For example, the sentence "Frogs eat insects" is a fact. This is information that can be looked up. However, the sentence "Frogs are handsome" is an opinion. This is a sentence that tells what a person thinks about frogs.

Read the following sentences and decide whether they are facts or opinions. After each sentence, write an "F" on the line if the sentence is a fact, or write an "O" if it is an opinion.

1. All toads are frogs, but not all frogs are toads._____

2. Amphibians lead double lives, in the water when they're young and out of the water when they're adults._____

3. Frogs and toads are ugly._____

4. Frogs were some of the first creatures to live on land._____

5. An amphibian's body temperature changes along with the air temperature around it._____

6. Frogs and toads are amphibians._____

7. Amphibians are really weird animals._____

8. Some amphibians bury themselves in the mud and hibernate through the winter._____

9. Amphibians make good pets._____

10. The sacs under a frog's chin help make its voice louder when it sings._____

11. Amphibians drink water in through their skin._____

12. There are over 3,000 different kinds of frogs living all over the world._____

13. Frogs and toads sound terrible when they sing._____

14. Salamanders are better than frogs because salamanders have tails._____

15. Amphibians need to stay in damp places to keep their skin moist._____

16. Frogs have smoother skin than toads._____

17. Tadpoles have gills; frogs have lungs._____

18. Newts are cute._____

My Frog and Toad Mini-Book

Use the boxes below to write and illustrate a cartoon picture book about Frog and Toad. To make your mini-book, cut along the solid lines. Fold down, in half, along the horizontal dashed line. Fold in half again along the vertical dashed line.

_____

_____

Ɛ

_____

_____

Z

4

1   **My Frog and Toad Mini-Book**

_____

_____

What Time Is It?

1. Look at Toad's list of daily activities below.
2. Draw the hands on the clock to show what time Toad does each activity.
3. In the last box, write another activity and show the time.

Toad wakes up.	Toad eats breakfast.	Toad visits Frog.
8:00 A.M.	8:30 A.M.	9:30 A.M.
Frog and Toad go for a walk.	Frog and Toad eat lunch.	Toad takes a nap.
10:30 A.M.	12:00 noon	12:30 P.M.
Frog and Toad play leapfrog.	Toad goes home.	
1:30 P.M.	3:00 P.M.	

Amphibian Life Cycle

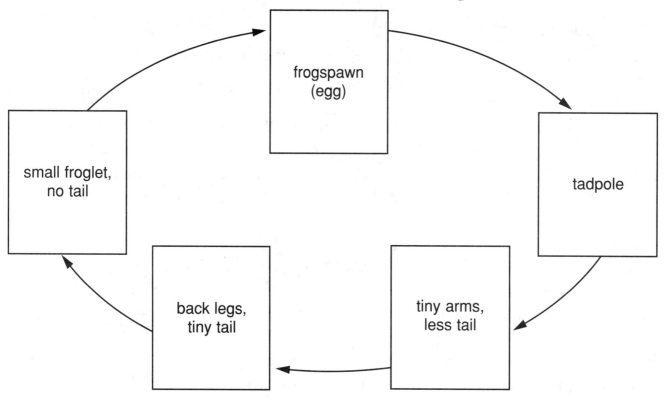

Frogs, toads, newts, and salamanders all belong to a group of animals called amphibians. An *amphibian* lays its eggs, called *spawn*, in water. The spawn are covered in a kind of jelly to protect them from other animal and bacteria. The tiny eggs soon hatch into very small animals called *tadpoles*. These tadpoles breathe through gills and don't look or act like their parents at all. At first, the tiny tadpoles eat plants, but soon they begin to feed on small water animals. They also begin to grow front legs. Soon their back legs begin to grow and their tails become shorter and eventually disappear. By this time, the tiny animal has developed lungs and no longer breathes through gills. The amphibian is now a small version of its adult parent. The salamander, newt, and toad will leave the ponds and rivers for a while, while the frog stays close to the water all its life. But all amphibians will one day come back to the water to begin the cycle again.

Activity

Cut out the boxes below. Glue them to the Amphibian Life Cycle chart above to show the correct order of the stages of development.

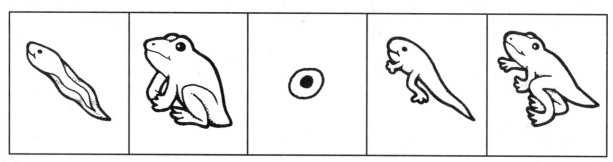

How Does Your Garden Grow?

Toad read a story, recited poems, sang songs, and played music for his seeds in order to help them grow faster. Use a ruler (with centimeters) to measure each of Toad's plants to the nearest centimeter. Write your answer below each plant.

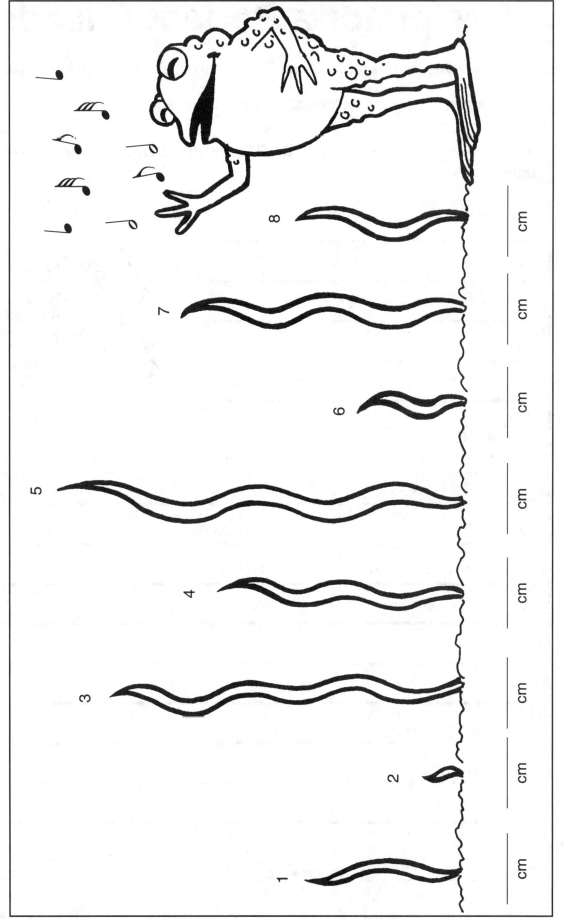

Recipe for a Perfect Friendship

Toad baked some cookies for his friend Frog. Think about what it takes to make a friendship.

Make up a recipe for a perfect friendship. Write it on the lines below.

——————— A Perfect Friendship ———————

Ingredients

————————————————————

————————————————————

————————————————————

————————————————————

Directions

————————————————————————————————

————————————————————————————————

————————————————————————————————

————————————————————————————————

————————————————————————————————

————————————————————————————————

————————————————————————————————

Bake at_____degrees for_____. Share it with
a friend.

Look Closer: Pond Life
Look Closer: River Life

by Barbara Taylor

Summary

Look Closer: Pond Life *and* Look Closer: River Life *beautifully detail the lives of the pond and river wildlife with captivating pictures and informative text. Students will delight in Frank Greenaway's photography and Barbara Taylor's clear writing style as they explore these fascinating underwater worlds. Each book begins with a close-up overview of the pond or river community. Each additional page highlights one of the many kinds of wildlife students may find in these bodies of water.*

The outline below suggests a plan for using activities presented in the unit. You may adapt the ideas to fit your own classroom situation.

Sample Plan

Lesson 1

- Begin reading *Look Closer: Pond Life*.
- Start Pond and River Watchers' Diary. (page 32)
- Create water adventure stories. (pages 33 and 34)
- Write about Sounds of the River. (pages 47 and 48)
- Play Lost Ducklings and River and Pond Relays. (page 73)

Lesson 2

- Continue reading *Look Closer: Pond Life*.
- Complete Pond and River Crossword. (page 35)
- Continue Pond and River Watchers' Diary. (page 32)
- Make pond and river food chain mobiles. (pages 36 and 37)
- Learn about The Amazing Water Cycle. (pages 39-41)

Lesson 3

- Begin reading *Look Closer: River Life*.
- Continue Pond and River Watchers' Diary. (page 32)
- Solve River Distance Math problems. (page 38)
- Choose related writing activities from Journal Topics. (page 42)
- Create a newspaper about pond and river life. (page 52)
- Learn the parts of a trout. (page 65)
- Follow directions on page 67 to make and display Paper Bag Ducks.

Lesson 4

- Continue reading *Look Closer: River Life*.
- Complete Pond and River Watchers' Diary. (page 32)
- Continue writing activities from Journal Topics. (page 42)
- Create class big books about pond and river life. (pages 43 and 44)
- Write haiku poems about pond and river life. (page 51)
- Make Metamorphosis Bracelets. (page 66)
- Play River and Pond Trivia Game. (pages 76-78)

Overview of Activities

Setting the Stage

1. *Look Closer: Pond Life* and *Look Closer: River Life* are excellent resources to use in conjunction with *All Eyes on the Pond*. Introduce the books by reviewing what the students have learned so far about ponds. Explain to students that the format of the Look Closer series allows them to take close up views of the pond and all its inhabitants.

2. Discuss food chains and how every plant and animal contributes to the careful balance of life in the pond. Have students make mobiles (pages 36 and 37) to demonstrate what a pond food chain might look like.

3. Ask students what they think makes a river different from a pond. If possible, expose students to *Where the River Begins* by Thomas Locker (Dial Books Young, 1984). This is the story about two boys' journey from the mouth of the river to its beginning in a small pond.

4. Take a trip to a local pet store or, if your community has one, your local water garden and view some of the pond animals up closely.

Enjoying the Books

1. Begin *Look Closer: River Life*, reading daily to meet and discuss the animals introduced in the book. Do the same with *Look Closer: Pond Life*. Introduce information and activities (see Sample Plan and Overview of Activities) throughout the unit at appropriate times throughout the reading of the books.

2. Create a word bank in the classroom. Add new vocabulary to the list and discuss their meanings as you come across them in the text. Encourage the students to create their own picture dictionaries as they work on their word banks. Have them decide on a word meaning and a sentence for each term, and illustrate each term. These can also be added to their All Eyes on the Pond and River pocket folders.

3. Have students use the Pond and River Watchers' Diary on page 32 to describe each new animal they meet as you read the Look Closer books. As students learn each of the animals in the pond, have them focus not only on the animal but also on its importance in the pond community.

4. Publish a class water adventure book using the information and directions on pages 33 and 34.

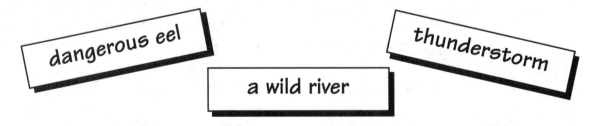

5. Have students create their own newspaper using the format on page 52. Each child chooses an animal, names it, creates an exciting headline (e.g. Tracy Trout Missing Since Friday, Wally Water Strider Walks on Water) and writes an article about the latest pond happenings, using the 5 W's (who, what, when, where, why or how). Students can use the information and activities from this unit as well as other sources to research their articles.

Overview of Activities *(cont.)*

Enjoying the Book *(cont.)*

6. Extend students' knowledge of pond and river life with the crossword puzzle on page 35. Provide dictionaries or other resources for students who need to look up the words in the word bank.

7. Read about Metamorphosis and construct Metamorphosis Bracelets on page 66.

8. Students can practice measuring distances as they read the story and solve the problems on page 38.

9. Introduce the water cycle (page 39)and discuss how it influences rivers and ponds. Have students complete the activities on pages 40 and 41. Ask students to share their experiment results and water cycle wheels.

10. Have students brainstorm the names of sounds of river animals (page 47). Then, ask students to use this information to write river sounds poetry. As an extension, write Haiku poetry about pond or river life. After introducing students to the Haiku format, create a word bank to be used for the poetry. Students can choose words from the word bank to write their own Haiku poetry.

11. Complete the Itchyology Isn't Icky activity on page 65. Label the parts of a trout. As an extension, have students research to discover more about the function of each part.

Extending the Books

1. As a culmination to the section activities, have students play the River and Pond Trivia Game on pages 76–78.

2. Have students write letters to the National Wildlife Federation, asking for information on various rivers and aquatic wildlife. This non-profit organization appreciates when you send a stamped, self-addressed envelope with your request.

   National Wildlife Federation
   8925 Leesburg Pike
   Vienna, VA, 22184-0001

3. Students can create panel drawings of the river's journey. For each student cut a 6" x 18" (15 cm x 46 cm) piece of construction paper and fold it into fourths. At the top of each panel, students write one portion of the following sentence: "A still pond trickled into a larger river that trickled into the deep, blue sea." Students then illustrate each part of the river's journey from the pond on the first panel through the river on the middle two panels to its ending in the deep, blue sea on the fourth panel.

4. Create a pond and river bulletin board, using yarn and butcher paper to show a river's journey around the classroom to an area designated the deep, blue sea. As the study continues, students may create art projects, drawings, and paintings illustrating the various wildlife to place in the river and along the riverbank.

5. Enjoy some of the Pond Food Festival treats on pages 74 and 75.

Pond and River Watchers' Diary

Your class will take an imaginary trip to the pond. Describe one animal you meet each day.
What does it look, sound, and feel like? To the right, draw a picture of each animal.

On_____I went to the pond

and saw a_____

_____

_____.

On_____I went to the pond

and saw a_____

_____

_____.

On_____I went to the pond

and saw a_____

_____

_____.

On_____I went to the pond

and saw a_____

_____

_____.

Create a Water Adventure

Cut the following ideas into strips and place them in three paper bags, one labeled character, one labeled setting, and one labeled problem. Have students choose one strip from each bag and write a story about it. Publish the stories in a class book.

Character	Setting	Problem
rambunctious rat	bottom of the pond	caught in a trap
slithering snake	a wild river	a flood
toothless turtle	rotting log	a fire
fat croaking frog	beside the river	a motorboat
dangerous eel	in the sky	accident
tri-colored trout	on the banks of the pond	an unidentified shadow
daring dragonfly	in a burrow	floating object
careful crayfish	the mouth of the river	thunderstorm
spirited sparrow	shady pond	pollution

Create a Water Adventure *(cont.)*

See page 33 for directions.

Character	Setting	Problem
tiny tadpole	stems of plants	hot, hot sun
speedy water strider	surface of the pond	hard rain
bumpy toad	muddy bottom	pond drying up
two busy beavers	quiet pond	floodwaters
pokey pond snail	long lily root	hungry bullfrog
sleepy newt	bark of dead tree	furious windstorm
waddling duck	rushes near the shore	chasing child
long water scorpion	cluster of lily pads	boy with a jar
striped salamander	soft mud	solid ice surface

Pond and River Crossword

Use the word bank to write the answers to the sentences in the crossword puzzle. Draw a line through each word as you use it only one time.

Word Bank

tadpoles
carnivores
pollution
mammals
herbivores
compound
amphibian
spawn
predator

Across

3. An_____is an animal that can live both in and out of water.

5. Dragonflies see out of_____eyes.

7. After they hatch from eggs, frogs begin their lives as_____.

8. _____are warm-blooded animals that have fur and breathe through their lungs.

9. Animals that eat plants are called_____.

Down

1. Frogs eat small insects. Frogs are_____.

2. Scientists call amphibians' eggs_____.

4. _____harms our ponds and rivers.

6. A_____is a meat-eating hunter.

Pond Food Chain Mobile

Pond and river animals need to eat other animals and plants to stay healthy. This is one example of a food chain pyramid. Cut out the shapes, and attach them onto string to create a food chain mobile that shows how each group depends on each other for survival.

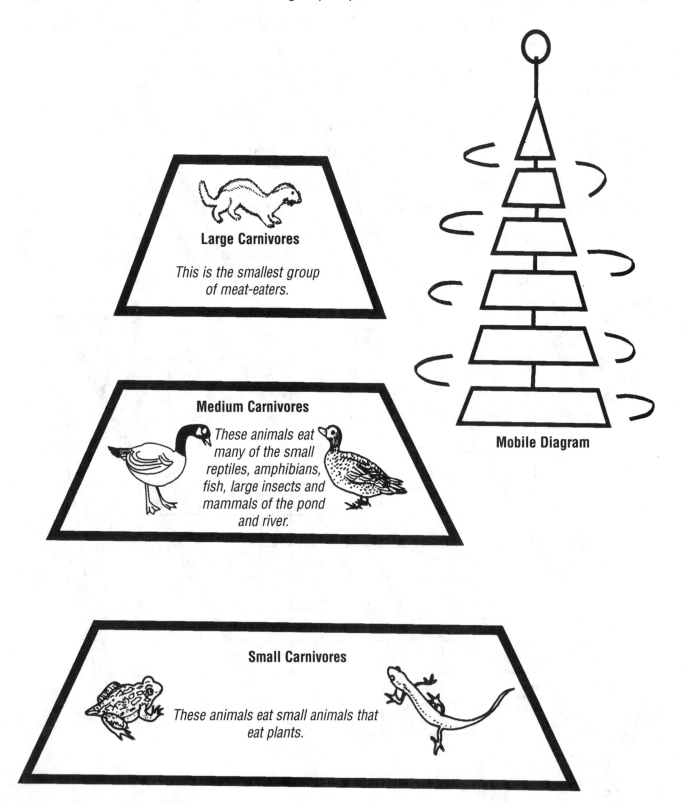

Large Carnivores

This is the smallest group of meat-eaters.

Mobile Diagram

Medium Carnivores

These animals eat many of the small reptiles, amphibians, fish, large insects and mammals of the pond and river.

Small Carnivores

These animals eat small animals that eat plants.

Pond Food Chain Mobile *(cont.)*

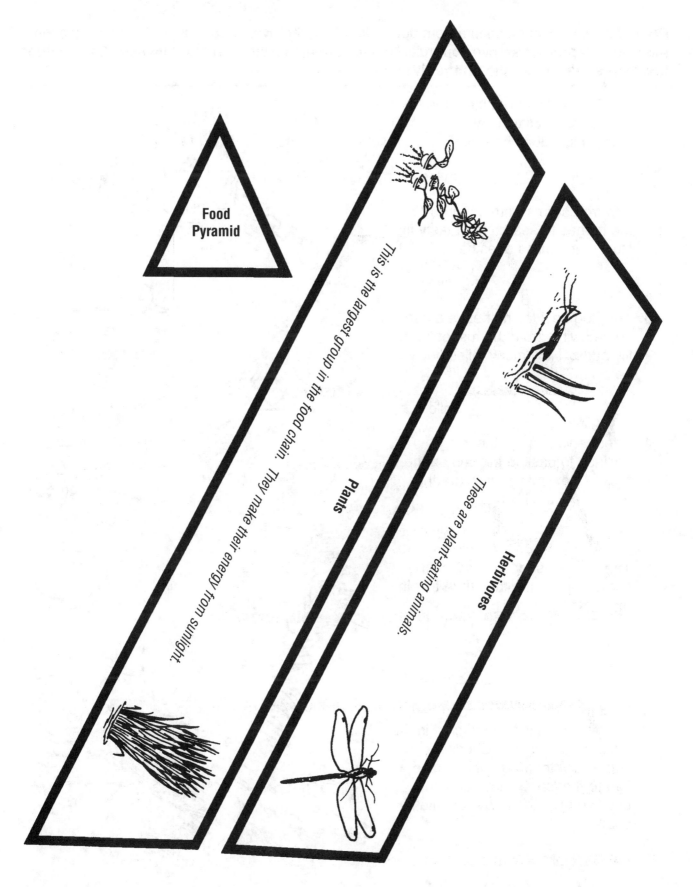

Food
Pyramid

This is the largest group in the food chain. They make their energy from sunlight.

Plants

These are plant-eating animals.

Herbivores

River Distance Math

Cut out the frog and move him from dot to dot along the river according to the information in the following problems. Use your ruler to measure the distance the frog travels. **One inch on the map equals one mile on the river.**

1. The frog swims from the turtle to the duck for a little chat. How many miles does he swim?

   _____miles

2. The frog swims from the duck to the rushes to search for a tasty fly. How many miles does he swim?

   _____miles

3. The frog decides he needs a nap, so he swims from the rushes to the lily pads. How many miles does he swim?

   _____miles

4. After he wakes up, the frog decides to bask in the sun on the rocks. How many miles are the rocks from the lily pad?

   _____miles

5. The frog feels too hot in the sun, so he hops along the shore to join the crayfish for a dip in the water. How far is the crayfish from the rocks?

   _____miles

6. It's time for the frog to go to bed. He swims to his favorite spot in the river. Where is it? (Choose a spot.) Cut the frog out and glue him to that spot. How far is the crayfish from the frog's favorite spot?

   _____miles

The Amazing Water Cycle

Did you know that the earth uses the same water over and over again? The water you use to wash your bike may be the same water a dinosaur drank many, many, many years ago! Hard to believe, but it's true. The water we drink, bathe in, and wash things with doesn't disappear once it travels down the drain. Water moves through different stages in a never-ending cycle. Read the descriptions of the stages below. Then create your own water cycle (page 40) and make a water cycle wheel (page 41).

Evaporation: Water molecules absorb the sun's heat and turn into water vapor. The vapor rises.

Condensation: Water vapor collects and turns to droplets. Clouds are formed as more and more water is absorbed. The clouds become heavy and begin to grow dark and ready to rain.

Precipitation: The heavy rain clouds release the water droplets. It's raining.

Accumulation: The rain that has fallen to earth collects into rivers, lakes, and the ocean.

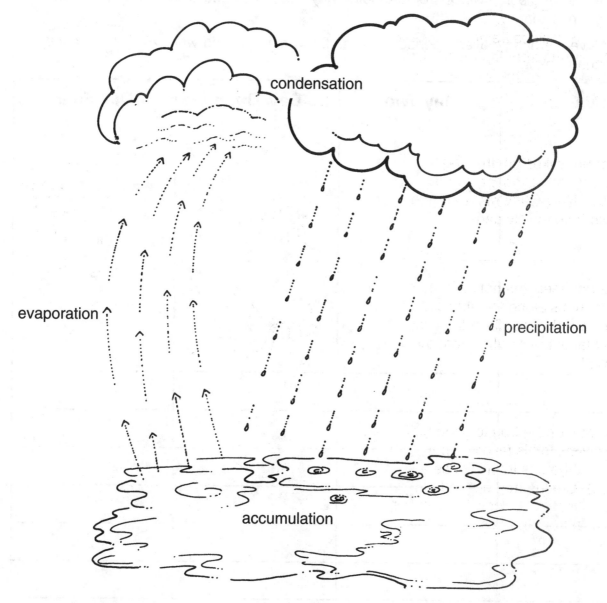

The Amazing Water Cycle *(cont.)*

See it for yourself! See the water cycle with your own eyes. Create your own cycle by following the directions outlined in the experiment below.

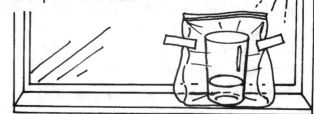

Materials

- 1 small plastic cup
- 1 "zippered" sandwich bag
- tape

Directions

1. Fill the plastic cup so it is about a quarter full.

2. Place the plastic cup in the corner of the bag and zip the bag closed.

3. Tape the baggie in a window or another sunny spot. Make sure the cup stays in an upright position.

4. Observe the baggie over a period of days. Draw pictures and write your observations in the chart below.

Day One	Day Two	Day Three	Day Four

The Amazing Water Cycle *(cont.)*

1. Color the pictures in the top circle.

2. Write the names of each stage on the lines.

3. Cut out the top circle.

4. Cut out the bottom circle along the dotted lines.

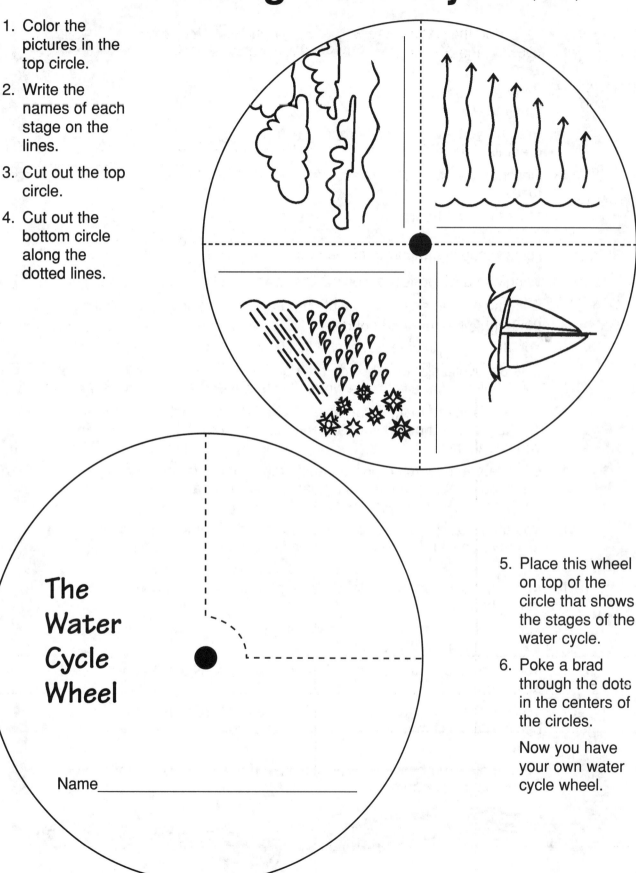

5. Place this wheel on top of the circle that shows the stages of the water cycle.

6. Poke a brad through the dots in the centers of the circles.

Now you have your own water cycle wheel.

The Water Cycle Wheel

Name_____

Journal Topics

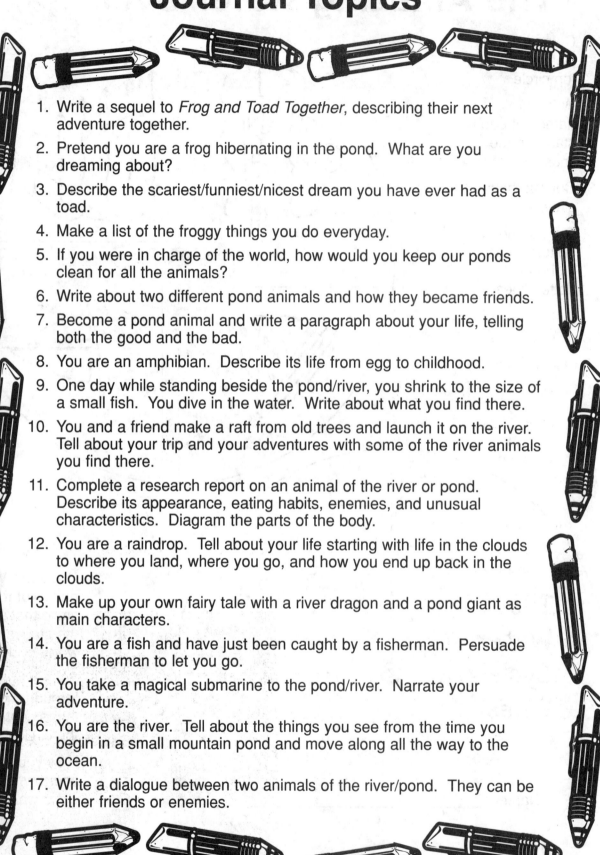

1. Write a sequel to *Frog and Toad Together*, describing their next adventure together.

2. Pretend you are a frog hibernating in the pond. What are you dreaming about?

3. Describe the scariest/funniest/nicest dream you have ever had as a toad.

4. Make a list of the froggy things you do everyday.

5. If you were in charge of the world, how would you keep our ponds clean for all the animals?

6. Write about two different pond animals and how they became friends.

7. Become a pond animal and write a paragraph about your life, telling both the good and the bad.

8. You are an amphibian. Describe its life from egg to childhood.

9. One day while standing beside the pond/river, you shrink to the size of a small fish. You dive in the water. Write about what you find there.

10. You and a friend make a raft from old trees and launch it on the river. Tell about your trip and your adventures with some of the river animals you find there.

11. Complete a research report on an animal of the river or pond. Describe its appearance, eating habits, enemies, and unusual characteristics. Diagram the parts of the body.

12. You are a raindrop. Tell about your life starting with life in the clouds to where you land, where you go, and how you end up back in the clouds.

13. Make up your own fairy tale with a river dragon and a pond giant as main characters.

14. You are a fish and have just been caught by a fisherman. Persuade the fisherman to let you go.

15. You take a magical submarine to the pond/river. Narrate your adventure.

16. You are the river. Tell about the things you see from the time you begin in a small mountain pond and move along all the way to the ocean.

17. Write a dialogue between two animals of the river/pond. They can be either friends or enemies.

Big Book Ideas

Primary children love to create their own versions of favorite literature books. These books often become classroom favorites and wear out by the end of the year from frequent use. Have your class create their own big book version of *All Eyes on the Pond*, and it is sure to become a classroom "classic."

Materials

- 12" x 18" (30 x 46 cm) white construction paper
- pencils, crayons, glue or paste, and scissors
- 12" x 18" (30 x 46 cm) blue construction paper
- blue tempera paint
- paint brushes

Directions

1. Brainstorm pond animals and their characteristics.

2. Chart the following sentence frame.

My eyes are on the pond.
I see a_____with_____.
What do you see?

3. Have each child choose an animal and its characteristics and complete the sentence frame.

4. Give each child a large piece of white construction paper on which to draw his or her pond animal. Encourage the children to use the whole piece of paper for their drawings.

5. After they have drawn their pond animals have students color the animals **as darkly as possible with crayons** and cut them out.

6. Give each student a blue sheet of construction paper to glue the pond creature on.

7. Thin blue tempera paint with water to create a wash, and have each child paint over the whole picture. The darkly crayoned areas should resist the paint and give the picture a watery feel. It is helpful to have lots of paper towels on hand to blot off excess paint.

8. When the pond paintings are dry, the children can recopy their sentence frames on sentence strips and glue them to the pond paintings.

9. Compile all of the students' pages into a classroom big book that is sure to be read often!

Big Book Ideas *(cont.)*

The ABC's of Pond and River Life

Have the children use their knowledge to write a pond and river ABC Book. Have the class brainstorm all the pond and river animals they can think of to fit each letter of the alphabet. The students will probably have to use research books to come up with animals for the more difficult letters. An excellent book to use for this activity is *The Frog Alphabet Book*. Each student then selects an animal and researches, writes a paragraph, and draws a picture of it. All of the students' work can then be compiled into an original ABC Book.

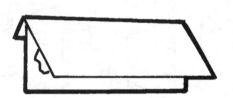

The Pond and River Riddle Book

Each student creates a picture of a pond plant or animal and glues a flap over the picture to conceal it. Below the picture, the student writes three clues about the plant or animal without naming it. The student then closes the riddle with the question, "What am I?" The reader can lift the flap and check his or her answer to the riddle.

Pond and River Math Books

Each student writes and illustrates his or her own story problem using addition, subtraction, multiplication, and/or division. At the close of his or her story, each student needs to solve the problem and write a number sentence stating the answer. A good closing technique is to have the students then state their answers in complete sentences.

Example: Frieda Frog ate two mouthfuls of flies. Each mouthful contained four flies. She then went to Daphne Duck and ate another fly for dessert. For a bedtime snack, she ate two more. How many flies did Frieda eat in all?

$2 \times 4 = 8$ $\qquad$ $8 + 1 + 2 = 11$ flies

Frieda Frog ate 11 flies in all.

Alliteration Books

Each student picks a pond plant or animal and writes a sentence about it. The trick is that every word in the sentence has to begin with the same letter. Sometimes it is helpful if the children can use the words like, it, is, and, or, a, etc., in their sentences. Dictionaries are also very helpful. This is an excellent way to encourage children to use new vocabulary words. These sentences usually become quite silly, and the students will have a great time illustrating them. These are also wonderful sentences to use for cursive writing or printing practice.

44

Lily Pad Compounds

Directions:

Cut out the lily pad pieces below. Use them to form compound words. Glue the lily pads onto the pond.

lily   water   dragon   weed   tail   gill

cat   duck   blue   pad   fly   fowl

Write a Letter

_____

_____

_____

Dear_____,

_____

_____

_____

_____

_____

_____

_____

_____

_____

_____

_____

_____

_____

_____

_____

_____

_____

Sounds of the River

Close your eyes and imagine that you are sitting on the bank of a river one sunny afternoon. At first you hear nothing but the sound of your own breathing, but gradually you begin to notice other sounds—quiet sounds, the wind is rustling; loud sounds, geese are honking; funny sounds, frogs are croaking. In fact, the river is alive with sounds, almost as if Nature is playing her very own symphony.

Brainstorm the names of the river animals, the sounds they make, and where they live in the river. **Chart what you imagine** in the columns below. An example is given. When you're done, use your chart and page 48 to write a beautiful poem about the sounds of the river.

Animal	Sound	Location
frog	croaking	lily pads

Sounds of the River *(cont.)*

Study the sample word chart below. Fill in the River Sounds word chart with your own names of river animals, sounds, and locations. When you are finished, you will have written a lovely poem that describes the musical sounds of the river.

River Sounds—Sample

I hear the sounds of the river,

(Animal)	(Sound)		(Place)
frogs	croaking	on the	lily pads
ducks	quacking	in the	water
water striders	whispering	on the	surface
dragonflies	flitting	in the	reeds

I hear the sounds of the river.

River Sounds

I hear the sounds of the river,

_____

_____

_____

_____

I hear the sounds of the river.

Water Poetry

Poetry is a wonderful way to entice children into creatively expressing their ideas about the information they are learning. Use the poetry suggestions below and on page 50 in your pond and river study. It is helpful for students to brainstorm words and phrases about ponds and rivers prior to composing their poems.

A **diamante** is a diamond-shaped poem about opposites. First, have each child choose a pair of pond or river opposites and then create a diamond-shaped poem following this pattern:

Lines 1 and 7 state the opposites.

Lines 2 and 6 state two adjectives that describe the opposite closest to it.

Lines 3 and 5 state "ing" words that tell about the opposite closest to it.

Line 4 contains four nouns. The first two nouns describe the first opposite. The second two nouns describe the second opposite.

Tadpole
Tiny, Green
Wriggling, Swimming, Eating
Gills, Tail, Lungs, Legs
Hopping, Croaking, Hiding
Bulbous, Eye-popping,
Frog

Color similes compare unlike things that are similar only in their color.

Line 1 asks the question, "What color is the river?"

Lines 2 through 5 answer the question with something similar in color only.

Line 6 concludes, "These are the colors of the river."

What color is the river?
What color is the river?
Blue like the heron's shimmering feathers,
Green like the mallard's shiny throat,
Brown like the cattail's velvety head,
Silver like the trout's glistening belly,
These are the colors of the river.

Shape Poems are poems written in the shape of the poem's topic. First, students draw a very simple outline of their favorite pond or river animal. Then they write descriptive words or phrases about that animal all around their shape.

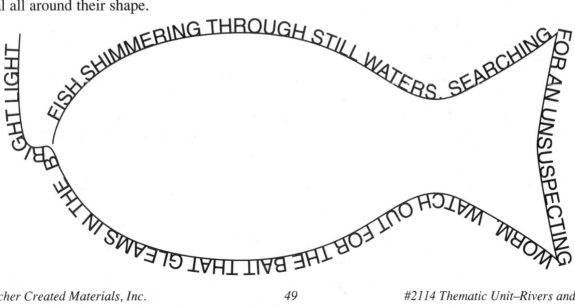

Water Poetry *(cont.)*

Life cycle poetry allows children to select a pond or river animal and write a poem from that animal's perspective. The students describe what they did as that animal when they were young and what they can do now.

Butterfly

When I was young I moved on many tiny legs,
Now I fly with colorful wings.
When I was young I munched and crunched on stalks and leaves,
Now I drink sweet nectar.
When I was young I lived amongst the creepers and crawlers,
Now I flit with the hummers.
When I was young I was the "ugly duckling,"
Now I am the "beautiful swan."

Favorite word poems line up at the colons. The students select five favorite words from their study on ponds and rivers. They write the words in list format. Next to each word, the students write a phrase that explains why the word is a favorite or a "keeper" for them.

Pond Favorites

Frog:	An aquatic songbird.
Dragonfly:	The closest thing to fairy wings.
Trout:	A fighter, swims upstream to lay its eggs.
Heron:	Beautiful blue bird from the heavens.
Pond:	Home, sweet home!

Haiku poems are usually written about nature. The first and third lines contain five syllables, and the second line contains seven. Even though the finished poem usually sounds quite simple, this particular form of poetry can be quite difficult for children to write. Since children find hearing the number of syllables the most challenging aspect of this poetry, **first brainstorm** a list of pond or river words on the chalkboard. Explain to students what a syllable is and clap out syllabic sounds. **Second, categorize** the words on the board by tapping out one-, two-, three-, or four-syllable words for the Haiku Word Bank on the following page. Have the students tap out and then cross off each word as they use it. This ensures against repeated words in their haikus.

Watery Baby

Watery baby
Swims through the dark murky pond
Soon will be a frog

Haiku Word Bank

1-Syllable Words	2-Syllable Words	3-Syllable Words	4-Syllable Words	5-Syllable Words

Water Gazette

| Daily News | Date | cents |

Photo by:

Sports   **Weather**

Problems to "Pond"er

The pond is an exciting community filled with many different animals, big and small. Use your math skills to discover just how busy pond life can be.

1.

Three little frogs hopped onto a log. They were joined by eight more. How many frogs sat on the log together?

_____

2.

Seven fireflies flew over the pond. Six other fireflies saw their light and joined their friends. How many fireflies were there in all?

_____

3.

Four spotted salamanders crawled along the bank of the river. Four more salamanders basked on a rock in the sun. How many salamanders were at the river?

_____

4.

Three mother ducks each laid four speckled eggs at the edge of the water. How many eggs were there?

_____

5.

Fourteen mosquitoes buzzed along the river bank. A snapping turtle ate eight of them. How many were left?

_____

6.

Eighteen tiny minnows swam together in the bog. Eleven swam off in another direction. How many minnows were left in the bog?

_____

7.

Eleven geese stopped at the pond for a sip of cool, clean water on their journey south. Four of the geese decided to stay there for the winter. How many geese flew away?

_____

8.

Two little girls went fishing at the river. Before long, each little girl had caught five fish. How many fish did they catch in all?

_____

Graph Your Favorite Animal

Materials

- 3" x 3" (8 cm x 8 cm) blank pieces of paper
- graph or butcher paper chart with headings for pond animals

Have children color a picture of their favorite pond animal on the squares and glue them to a chart. (See sample below.) Remind students to build from the bottom of the graph up.

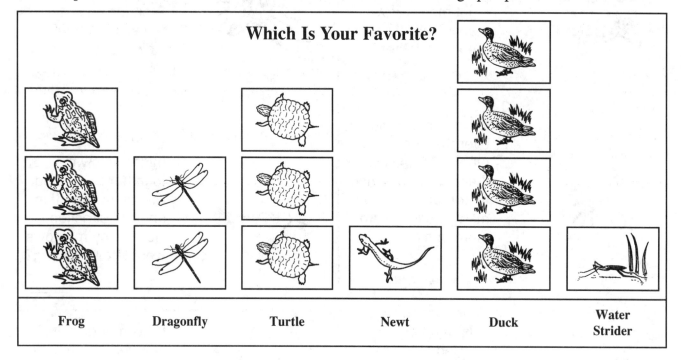

Which Is Your Favorite?

| Frog | Dragonfly | Turtle | Newt | Duck | Water Strider |

Discussion Questions

1. Which animal did most students choose? (*duck*)
2. Which animals did the fewest students choose? (*newt, water strider*)
3. How many more students chose frogs than water striders? (*2 more students*)
4. How many fewer students chose_____than_____? (*your choice*)
5. How many students chose_____and_____together? (*your choice*)

Other Graphing Activities

1. What is your favorite cookie?
2. What time do you go to bed?
3. Who can jump the farthest?
4. Was the last dream you had scary, funny, or happy?
5. Would you kiss a toad to get what you want?
6. Which do you like best, frogs or toads?
7. Which animal is the slimiest?

Cooperative Cookie Math

This beautiful class math book makes an excellent follow-up to "The Cookies" in *Frog and Toad Together*. Each group of students will be responsible for adding one illustrated math problem, the word problem, and the number sentence to their page of the math book.

Group students into seating arrangements of 3 to 4 students per table. Depending on the math abilities of your students, each group will use 1 to 4 copies of the cookie handout on page 56. Provide 1 sheet per table for addition and subtraction, 1 sheet per child for multiplication and division, scissors, crayons, writing materials, and 1 (12" x 18"/30 cm x 56 cm) sheet of construction paper.

Introduce the activity by asking children what their favorite cookies are. (You may want to graph responses as suggested on page 54.) Ask them how many like chocolate chip cookies.

Explain that today, as a class, they will be working together as a group to create a very special cookie math book that, when finished, will be placed in the classroom library for others to learn from. Their group will make at least one page.

Demonstrate one to two examples on the overhead, using cutout cookies, guiding and soliciting wording and answers from the children.

Addition
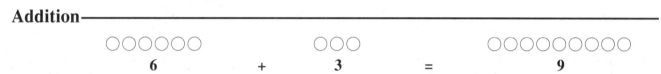

If Lindsay had six cookies and Ali gave her three cookies, how many cookies does Lindsay have all together?

Subtraction

If Casey had seven cookies and gave Kyle 2 cookies, how many cookies would she have left?

Multiplication
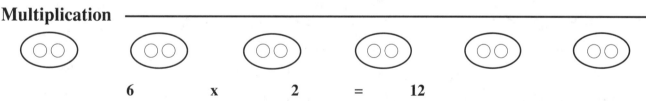

There are six children at your table. Each child has 2 cookies. How many cookies do you have all together?

Division
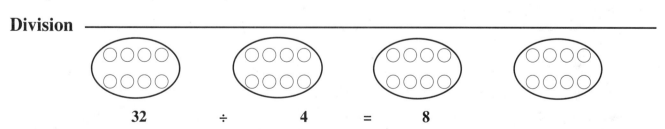

Paul brought 32 cookies for his friends at school. He will distribute them to four groups of children. How many cookies will each group get?

Cooperative Cookie Math *(cont.)*

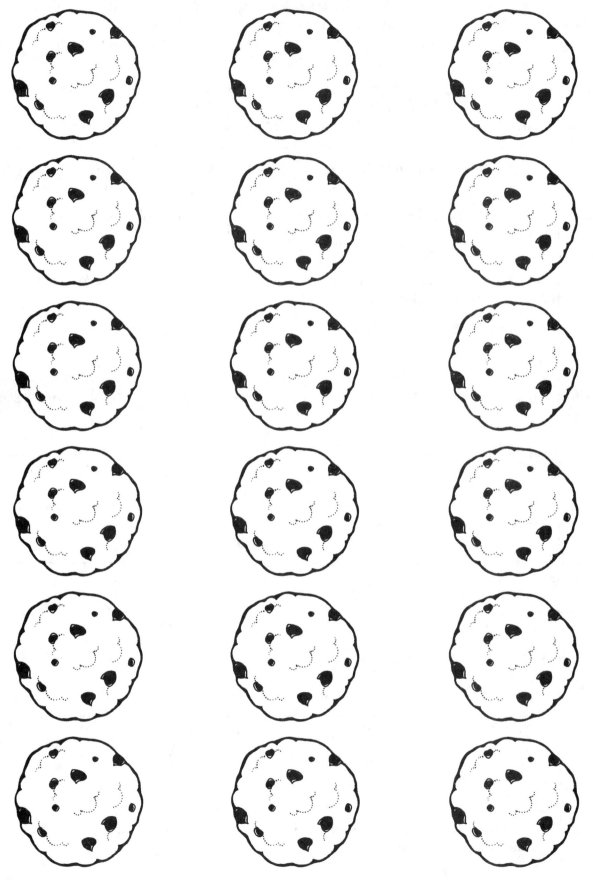

Leapfrog Math

Tina Toad, Freddie Frog, Bobby Bunny, Ricky Rat, Chester Cricket, and Nicky Newt held a jumping contest. Look at the graph and answer the questions below.

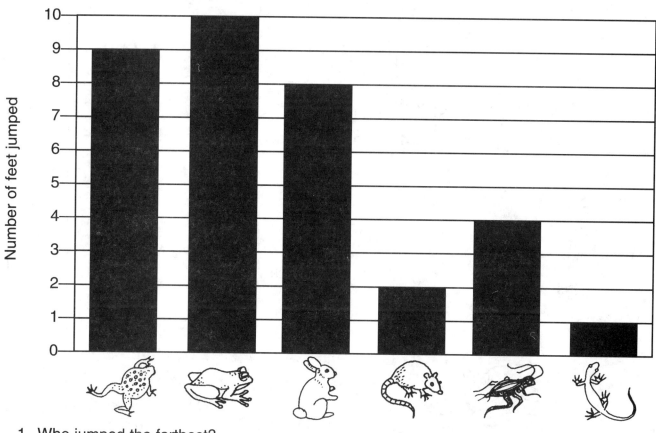

1. Who jumped the farthest?_____

2. How much farther did Bobby Bunny jump than Chester Cricket?_____

3. How far did the animals jump all together?_____

4. Who jumped the shortest distance?_____

5. How many animals jumped less than five feet?_____

6. How many jumped more than six feet?_____

7. How much farther did Freddie Frog jump than Tina Toad?_____

8. How far did the two top jumpers jump together?_____

Think about these and write your answers.

9. Why do you suppose the winning jumpers jumped so far?_____

10. Why didn't some of the animals jump very far at all?_____

Hold your own jumping contest with friends and graph your results.

Pond Directions

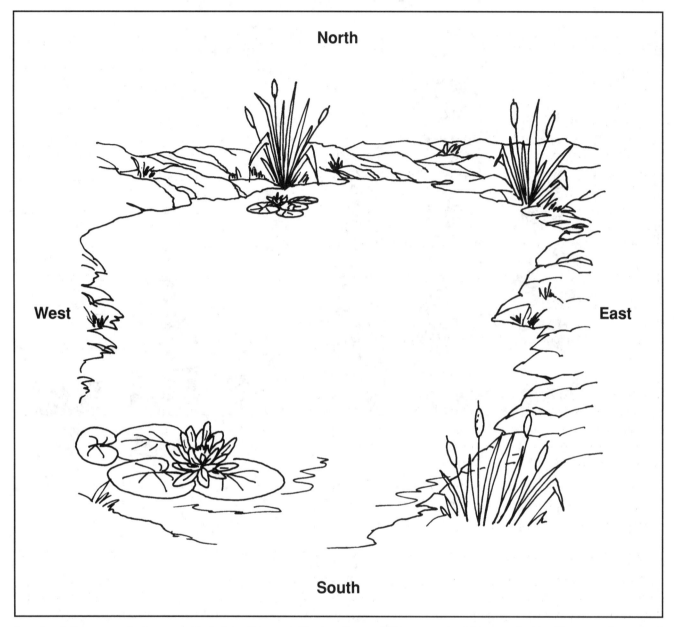

Look at the pond above. Point to the **north** section of the pond. Now point to the **east** part of the pond. Point to the **south**. Now point to the **west**. You are ready to begin.

Follow the directions below to show all the animals in the pond. When you finish you may color your pond map.

1. Draw a snapping turtle in the south section of the pond.

2. Draw a dragonfly over the north part of the pond.

3. Show a frog leaping off a lily pad into the pond in the east section of the pond.

4. Draw a school of fish in the west part of the pond.

5. Show a duck swimming in the south section of the pond.

6. Draw a bat flying over the east part of the pond.

Seasons of the Pond

The Pond in Spring ●

As winter ends the days gradually warm and grow longer. With the increase in daylight hours, pond plants begin their race for a place in the sun. Spring has arrived at the pond. The duckweeds and algae are among the first plants to show their growth because they're small and need little food. All around the pond and in the marshy areas along the river, irises, reeds, and other plants are beginning to unfold their green shoots and leaves. As the sun's warmth spreads through the water, animals in the weeds and in the mud at the bottom of the pond awaken. Frogs, toads, fish, and newts court, mate, and lay eggs. Their eggs soon hatch in the warmer water, and the energetic offspring set off in search of their next meal. The cold-blooded animals become more active as the water temperature rises, and with this increase in activity comes an increase in hunger. The pond is teeming with life in the spring. Finding food is much easier now than in the long cold winter.

The Pond in Summer ●

Summer is a time for pond plants to grow and become thick and lush. The amount of growth and kind of plant depends mainly on how much sunlight the pond receives. Only a large growth of plant life will provide the food, shelter, and places for nesting required by the pond animals.

In early summer, pond animals feed heartily and fatten up. Tadpoles, insect larvae, and other small creatures hungrily feed on the rich plant growth. These animals are also known as herbivores because they eat only plants. Larger animals such as newts and small fish feed on these smaller herbivores and also pond animals such as frogs, fish, and snails. These animals are also called carnivores because they eat only meat. In this way the pond food chain is created.

All plants and animals in the pond will eventually die, and this too helps the living creatures in the pond. Animal remains and droppings enrich the water by providing food for some animals and minerals for fresh plant growth. Nothing is wasted; everything is recycled in the pond.

The Pond in Autumn ●

As summer ends and the days grow shorter, the pond animals slow down and prepare for winter. Some of the smaller water creatures are busy laying eggs now, for these animals will die before the winter comes. Their eggs will hatch in the spring, bringing new life. Some types of ducks and geese fly south in the anticipation of the cold weather, while the animals that stay stuff themselves on ripe fruit. They are building up fat stores for the long winter that lies ahead.

Many of the pond plants that were green and lush in the spring and summer are drying out and dying now in the fall. But even as they die, insects, animals, and wind are scattering their seeds that will burst forth with new life in the spring.

The Pond in Winter ●

During the long cold days of winter, fish, water mollusks, and worms move to the deepest part of the pond where they won't be iced in. Their bodies cool off and slow down so they can survive with much less food and oxygen. Other small pond creatures lay eggs in the autumn before they die. The eggs lie dormant through the winter, and they hatch in spring. Frogs and toads find a protected place on land and hibernate until spring. Winter is a quiet, sleepy time at the pond.

Seasons of the Pond *(cont.)*

Comprehension Questions

Answer the following questions after reading the information on page 59.

1. What happens to the daylight hours and temperatures in spring?

   _____

   _____

2. As daylight hours increase and temperatures rise, how do pond animals and plants respond?

   _____

   _____

3. What is a pond food chain? Describe.

   _____

   _____

4. How do the remains of plants and animals help the pond environment?

   _____

   _____

5. What happens to pond plants and animals in the autumn? Describe.

   _____

   _____

6. Why is it easier for pond animals to find food in the spring than it is in the winter?

   _____

   _____

7. What do you do in the spring that is different from what you do in the winter?

   _____

   _____

8. How are you like a pond animal in the winter? How are you different?

   _____

When Is a Frog Not a Frog?

Complete the Venn diagram below to compare frogs and toads. In the section labeled **Frogs** list all the facts that apply only to frogs. In the section labeled **Toads** list all the things that are true of toads only. In the section labeled **Both**, show all the facts that are true of both frogs and toads.

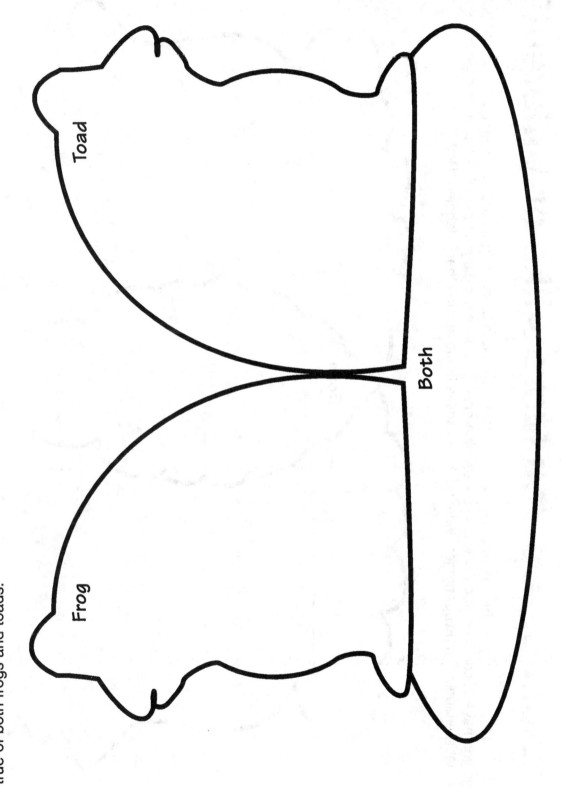

Toad

Frog

Both

Friends: Are You More Alike or Different?

Frog and Toad were very good friends who were alike in some ways and different in others. Choose a partner and talk about the things you have in common and the ways you are different. Complete the diagram below. Write your differences in the sections that are labeled with your names; write your similarities in the section that is labeled "Both."

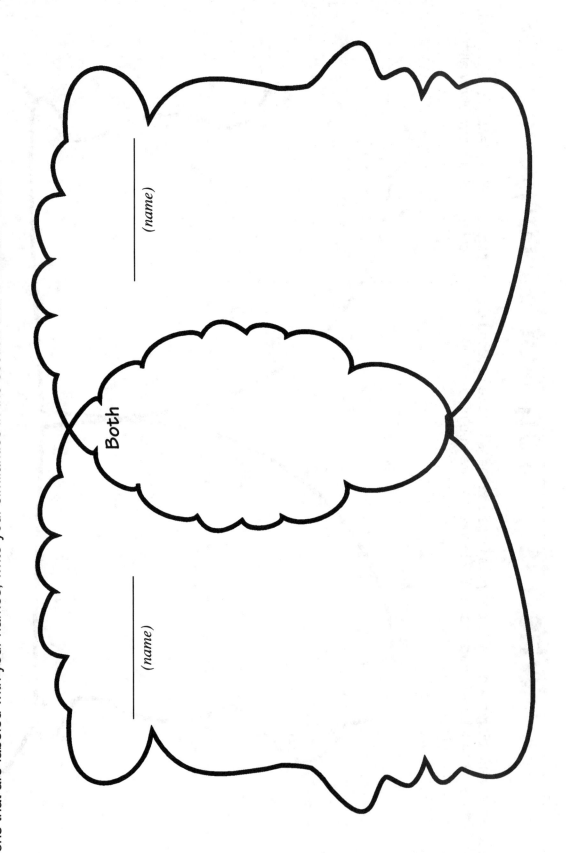

(name)

Both

(name)

Underwater Pond Scope

Make an underwater pond scope for your classroom pond or when exploring an outdoor pond.

Materials

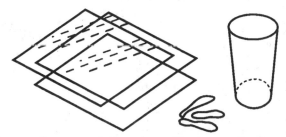

- 6" x 6" (15 cm x 15 cm) clear cellophane square
- rubber band or electrical tape
- Styrofoam or plastic cup

Cut the bottom out of the cup for the eyepiece. Cover the top of the cup with the cellophane and secure it with a rubber band or the electrical tape. Slowly scope the pond for an interesting underwater view. Draw what you see in the space below.

Make a Classroom Pond

Classroom Frog Pond

Materials

- tank
- fine gravel
- assorted sunning rocks
- several water weeds
- spawn or tadpoles

Create your own classroom frog pond. In April, search shallow ditches, ponds, and bogs for frogs, toads, spawn, or tadpoles. A small handful of tadpoles will be plenty. Froglets will mature after 12 weeks.

Directions

Prepare a large tub or tank with an inch (2.5 cm) layer of fine clean gravel and sand in the pond, building up to a sandy beach. Fill it about half full of water. Add rocks to climb on and small water plants for food and oxygen. Place it in a shady spot and observe it with small magnifying glasses. Five weeks after the spawn hatch, add mosquito larvae, cheese, or bacon for protein.

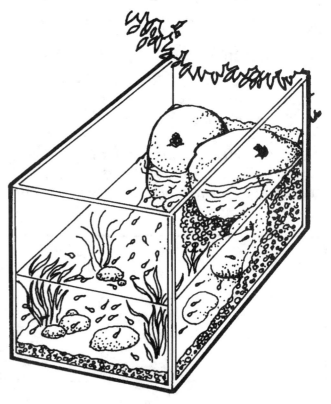

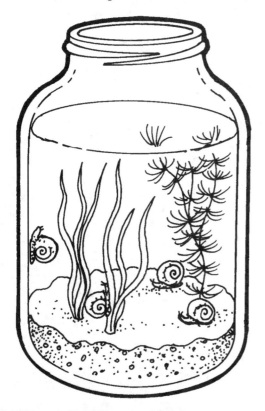

Snail Pond in a Jar

Materials

- a very clean, large jar
- gravel
- stalks of water weed (elodea or anacharis)
- two or three small pond snails

Directions

Thoroughly wash the gravel and place a layer at the bottom of the jar. Push a few sprigs of pond weed into the gravel. Slowly fill the jar almost to the top with pond water. Put the snails in the jar, fit the lid on loosely, and let it stand near a window. The water weeds provide food and oxygen for the snails. The snails in turn breathe out carbon dioxide which the plants need to make their fuel.

Ichthyology Isn't Icky

The trout is a beautiful, iridescent fish that lives in many of our freshwater lakes, ponds, and rivers. Just like its relative, the salmon, it swims upstream to lay its eggs. There are many different types of trout, including one kind known as the sea trout that lives in the ocean part of the year.

Look at the diagram of the golden trout and then read the statements below. The words in bold print are the names of the different parts of the trout. See if you can write the names on the correct lines next to the diagram of the trout.

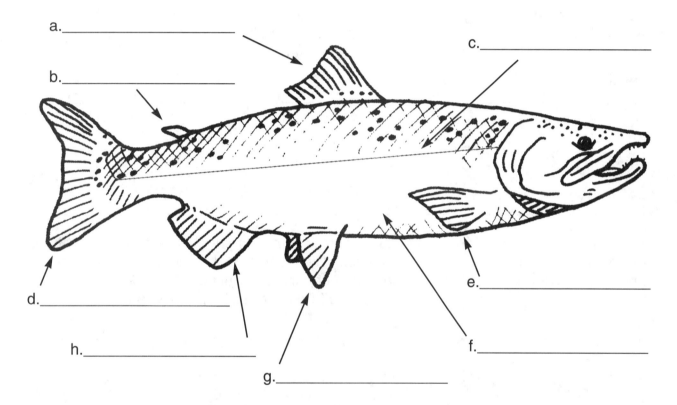

a._____

b._____

c._____

d._____

e._____

f._____

g._____

h._____

1. These fins are on the underside of the trout closest to its mouth. These are known as the **pectoral fins**. They help the trout swim upward or downward.

2. This line appears to divide the fish into two parts. It is known as the **lateral line**.

3. The iridescent **silver belly** of the trout helps it blend in with the water and hide from predators lurking in the water below.

4. The spiny **dorsal fin** is the larger fin that sits on the upper side of the trout.

5. A rainbow trout has brown spots on its **tail**, but a brown trout does not.

6. The soft **adipose fin** can be found between the trout's dorsal fin and the tail.

7. The large fin on the underside of the trout's body is known as the **anal fin**.

8. The small **ventral fin** is located between the trout's pectoral and anal fins.

After you have labeled the trout, use your silver and gold crayons to color your fish and give it a sparkling or iridescent effect.

Metamorphosis Bracelets

When many animals are born they look very different from their parents. These animals must go through a process called metamorphosis before they become adults. Metamorphosis is the process in which an animal changes from one form to a completely different form.

The animals below have all gone through metamorphosis. Choose one. Color the stages of its life on the strip below. Cut out the strip on the solid lines, glue it together, and slip it onto your wrist. When your friends ask about it, explain the process of metamorphosis.

Amphibians like the frog begin life as an egg. The egg hatches into a tadpole, a fish-like creature that soon loses its tail and grows arms, legs, and lungs. One day the tiny froglet is ready to leave the water, looking like a miniature version of its parent.

Another animal that goes through a metamorphosis is the butterfly. Butterfly eggs hatch into larvae which we call caterpillars. They look like fat worms. Most of the larvae feed on plants until they are ready to spin their pupa or chrysalis around their bodies. Their bodies change inside the pupa until one day the fully changed butterfly breaks free.

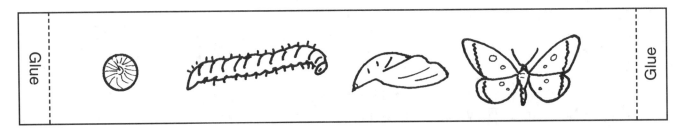

The dragonfly also completes a metamorphosis in its life. Dragonfly eggs hatch into larvae which are called nymphs. These nymphs feed on small insects, tadpoles, and tiny fish in the water for one to three years. Over this time, they shed their skins, or molt, up to 25 times before they are ready to leave the water. They climb up out of the water, shed their skins one more time, and an adult dragonfly emerges.

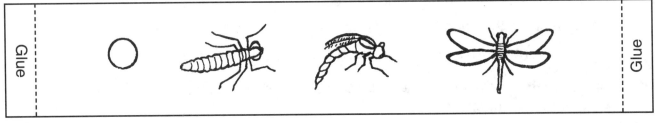

Art Projects

Froggy Pop-Up Puppet

Materials

- 16 Styrofoam cups
- pencils
- frog pattern (page 70)
- Easter grass
- google eyes

Directions:

1. Cut out one of the frog patterns, color it, and attach the google eyes with glue.

2. Attach the frog to the end of a pencil. Insert the pencil into a cup through the hole.

3. Fill the tumbler with colorful Easter grass.

The children can make their puppets jump by moving the pencil up and down through the hole.

Paper Bag Duck

Materials

- white paper lunch bags
- flower, lily pad, bill, wing, feet patterns (pages 70–72)
- 9-inch (23 cm) piece of colorful yarn
- newspaper

Directions

1. Crumple one piece of newspaper into a loosely packed ball. Place it in the bottom of the lunch bag.

2. Tie a piece of yarn tightly into a bow halfway down the bag so the bag is divided into two sections, head and body.

3. Crumple a smaller piece of newspaper into a tight, small ball and place it into the upper section of the bag. This forms the duck's head. Staple the top of the bag shut.

4. Color and cut out the lily pad and flower and glue then on the duck's head like a hat.

5. Color and cut out the bill pattern and affix it to the duck's face. Have the children use crayons to color the duck's eyes.

6. Color, cut out, and glue the feet to the bottom of the lunch bags.

7. Cut out the wings and attach them to the sides of the ducks.

Art Projects *(cont.)*

Paper Plate Frog

Materials

- small paper plates (dessert size)
- green tempera paint
- green construction paper (9" x 12"/23 cm x 30 cm)
- scraps of black, white, and red or pink construction paper

Directions

1. Each student needs to paint the front and back side of a paper plate with the green tempera paint. Let the plates dry thoroughly.

2. Have the children cut the green construction paper into four strips. Older children can measure their papers into four strips that are three inches (8 cm) wide. Cut a "V" section into one end of each strip to make them look more like frogs' feet. Fan-fold the legs to give them some "spring" action.

3. Students then fold their paper plates in half. Have them glue two of the legs onto the back of the plate (where the fold is) and two of the strips off to the sides.

4. Students use the black and white construction paper to make big eyes for the frog. They need to make a small fold at the bottom of each eye and apply glue there. Children attach the eyes to the top of the paper plate. The eyes should "pop" up.

5. Each child cuts a strip of red construction paper into a long, thin strip. This will be the frog's tongue. Students fan-fold the tongue and glue it inside the paper plate. The tongue should look like it is sticking out of the frog's mouth.

Tissue Paper Polliwog

Materials

- white construction paper (12" x 18"/ 30 cm x 46 cm)
- various shades of blue and green tissue paper
- starch
- black tempera paint
- paintbrushes

Directions

1. Distribute a piece of white construction paper to each child.

2. The students rip the tissue paper into long strips.

3. Then lay strips of tissue paper onto the construction paper; paint over it with starch.

4. Let the paper dry thoroughly.

5. Students trim any excess tissue from the edges of the construction paper.

6. The students use the black tempera paint to paint the silhouettes of tadpoles onto the tissue-covered construction paper.

Art Projects *(cont.)*

3-D Lily

Materials

- lily pad pattern below, one per student
- flower pattern (page 70), two per student
- toilet paper tubes, one per student
- scissors and glue

Directions

1. Reproduce the lily pad pattern below onto green construction paper and the flower pattern onto yellow or pink paper.

2. Have each student cut out one lily pad and two flowers.

3. The students place a dab of glue onto the back of one of the flowers and glue it in the center of the other flower, rolling the petals of the inner flower gently towards the center.

4. Have the children glue the lily onto the center of the lily pad. Allow it to dry.

5. Give each child a toilet paper tube. The student makes four vertical cuts down from the top of the tube at least one-third of the way down. The students bend back the flaps they have created on the tube and apply glue to each flap. The lily pad is then glued to the flaps. The tube now serves as a stand for the water lily.

Art Projects *(cont.)*

Patterns for Paper Bag Duck Flower and Froggy Pop-Up Puppet

Cut two for flower.

Glue to lily pad as directed on page 69.

Cut one for Froggy Pop-Up Puppet.

Art Projects *(cont.)*

Patterns for Duck Feet and Bill.

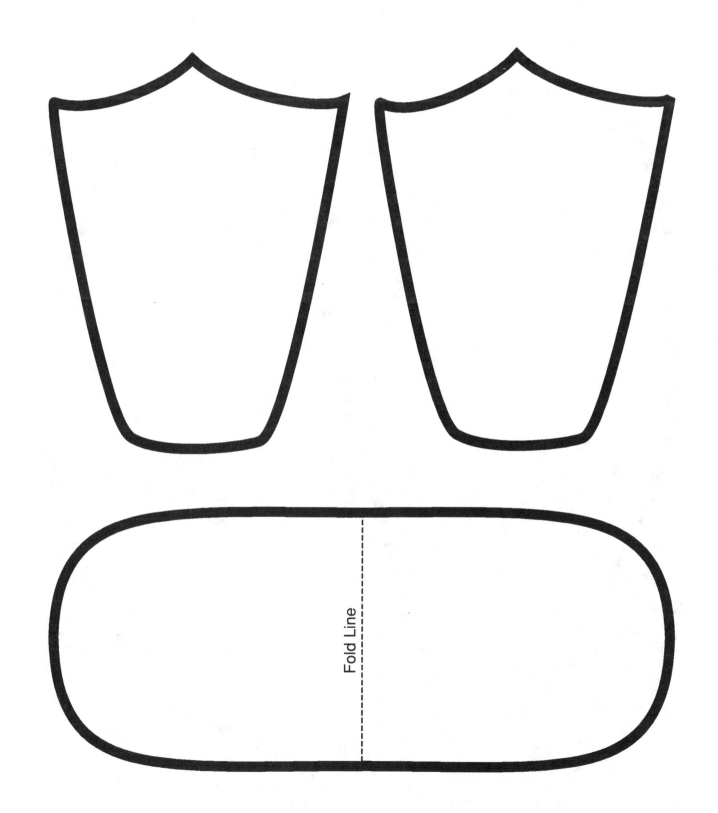

Fold Line

Art Projects *(cont.)*

Patterns for Duck Wings

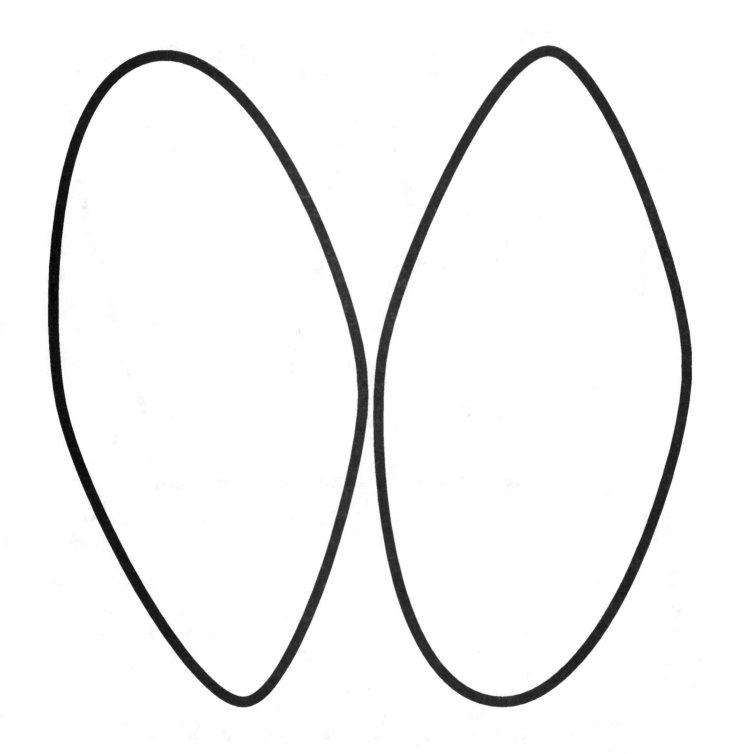

Pond Play

Lost Ducklings

This game can be saved for rainy days or used anytime during this study. Choose one child to be the Mother Duck. He or she leaves the room. While the Mother Duck is gone, the rest of the children (the *ducklings*) leave their seats and walk around the room. When the Mother Duck returns to the room, the teacher says, "The ducklings are lost. Please lead them safely home." The Mother Duck then tries to seat the ducklings in their own places; the object is to see how many he/she can seat correctly.

Frogs and Flies

Divide the class into two groups and designate a playing area. The first group, the Frogs, sit cross-legged around the playing area. The second group, the Flies, buzz around the Frogs. When the teacher blows the whistle, all flies must freeze. If a Frog can reach a Fly from his or her sitting position, the Fly must sit down and become a Frog. The game ends when all the Flies are caught.

River and Pond Relays

This game is a simple relay race with a new twist. Depending on class size, divide the students into teams of 4 to 8 players. Designate movements associated with pond or river animals for each leg of the relay, such as long steps for the water strider, running with arms out in flying motion for the dragonfly, duck walk, hopping frogs, and running backwards like a crayfish. When the signal is given, the first person in each team runs to the goal line, tags it, returns to the starting line, and tags the next person in line. The team that wins has all their players back in their original places, provided no one started before he was tagged.

Frog in the Pond

This game is played in a small area or outdoors. The child who is selected to be Frog sits cross-legged in the middle of a circle. The other players call, "Frog in the pond, can't catch me!" while stepping in and out of the circle, daring Frog to catch them. The frog tries to tag someone without leaving his or her sitting position. The first one tagged changes places with Frog.

Pond Food Festival

The following recipes are fun to integrate into your unit on ponds and rivers. "Mmm, Mmm, Mud!," "Ants on a Log," and "Pond Punch" work well with *All Eyes on the Pond* and the Look Closer books, while "Froggy Faces" seems especially well-suited for *Frog and Toad Together*.

Mmm, Mmm, Mud!

Equipment

- an electric mixer or blender
- large serving spoon
- 8-ounce (225 g) clear plastic cups, one per student
- 1 plastic spoon per student

Ingredients:

- chocolate pudding mix, enough to make ½ cup (125 mL) per student
- chocolate wafers or cookies, 2 per student
- candy worms, 1 or 2 per student

Directions

1. Make the pudding according to the package.
2. Spoon ½ cup (125 mL) of the pudding into each student's plastic cup.
3. Distribute two chocolate wafers and a gummy worm to each student.
4. Have the children sink their gummy worm into their chocolate pudding and top off their "mud" with a layer of "humus" or crumbled cookies.

The students will love eating the "mud" and hunting for the gummy worms with their spoons. Another enjoyable way to use this recipe is to hide the worm in each cup of pudding without the student's knowledge. The children add the cookie crumbs and then hunt for their ooey-gooey surprise.

Ants on a Log

Equipment

- plastic knives, one per student
- wax paper
- 10 to 12 small bowls (empty margarine tubs work well)

Ingredients:

- celery stalks cut into pieces
- peanut butter
- raisins

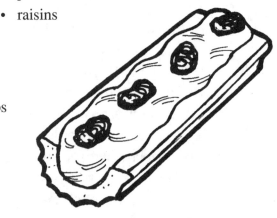

Directions

1. Cut the celery into pieces ahead of time.
2. Pass out a piece of wax paper to each child. This keeps the mess off their desks.
3. Distribute a small bowl of raisins and a small bowl of peanut butter to every group of three or four students.
4. Distribute the plastic knives.
5. Pass out two or three pieces of celery to each student.
6. Let each student fill up his or her "log" (celery) with "sap" (peanut butter) and "ants" (raisins.)

The students will enjoy going home and telling their parents about this nutritious snack!

Pond Food Festival *(cont.)*

Froggy Faces

Equipment

- plastic knives, one per student
- wax paper

Ingredients

- small colorful candy pieces
- black licorice strips cut into approximately 2" (5 cm) sections
- three or four tubs of white frosting
- green food coloring
- refrigerated sugar cookie dough, enough to make at least one cookie per student

Directions

1. Prior to class, slice and bake the sugar cookies according to the package directions.
2. Give each child one cookie on a piece of wax paper.
3. Mix a few drops of green food coloring into the frosting until it turns a convincing shade of "froggy green."
4. Give each group of four to five children a tub of frosting, a small container filled with m&m's®, and pieces of black licorice.
5. Let the students frost their cookies and use the candy to create "froggy faces." The black licorice works well for the frog's mouth.

Sometimes it's fun to list words that describe feelings on the chalkboard and challenge students to create expressions on their cookies that reflect particular emotions.

Pond Punch

Equipment

- two or three large pitchers
- a large mixing spoon
- plastic drink cups, one per student

Ingredients

- two or three large packages of yellow lemonade mix
- blue food coloring
- water

Directions

1. Pre-mix the lemonade, following directions on the package.
2. Squeeze a few drops of blue food coloring into the lemonade until the mixture turns a nice shade of murky green.
3. Sip and enjoy!

This recipe lends itself to a quick lesson on color.

Culminating Activity

River and Pond Trivia Game

Copy and cut out the trivia cards on pages 77 and 78. Give one card to each student. The person with the star on his or her card begins the game by standing and reading the riddle on the card. The student who has the answer to the first riddle stands up, reads it out loud, and reads the riddle on his or her card. The game progresses until all of the students have had a chance to read their riddles. The person who begins the game also ends the game with the answer to the last riddle appearing at the top of his or her card (next to the star).

ANSWER KEY

1. I am a small body of water that is home to many different kinds of plants and animals. (pond)
2. Each of my thick, heart-shaped leaves carries one flower and floats on the surface of the pond. (water lily)
3. I have large, powerful wings to hover over the pond while I search for my food. (dragonfly)
4. I began my life as a tadpole. I live mostly in the water. I have four legs, no tail, and smooth skin. (frog)
5. I have a large flat foot that I use to move slowly up and down pond plants in my search for food. (water snail)
6. I have webbed feet for swimming and a flexible neck for grabbing food underwater. My feathers are covered with an oily coating. (duck)
7. I have four webbed feet that help me swim, and I carry a hard, protective shell on my back. (turtle)
8. We are clumps of frogs' eggs that float on the surface of the pond. (jelly babies)
9. I am a six-legged insect that easily walks on the water's surface. (water strider)
10. I am a relative of the frog. I, too, was once a tadpole. Now, in addition to my four legs, I also have a tail. (salamander)
11. I have a streamlined body that's great for swimming quickly. I also have three sharp spines on my back. (stickleback)
12. I look like a tiny boat rowing across the surface of the water, but I am really an insect. My back legs look like oars. (water boatman)
13. I am a small, furry mammal with a very long tail. I live along the river bank and feed mainly on plants and berries. (water rat)
14. I am related to the crab or lobster. I have a protective outer shell called an exoskeleton. (crayfish)
15. I am related to the salmon. I also swim upstream to lay my eggs. (trout)
16. I am a tiny fish, only two inches (5 cm) long. I can lay up to 2,000 eggs. (minnow)

17. I have a long, smooth body that moves from side to side across the surface of the water. Some people think I look like an eel. (water snake)
18. I am a nocturnal mammal that flies low over the water to catch my favorite meal, insects. (bat)
19. My larvae hatch from eggs. I build a protective tube of sand and plant matter to protect their soft bodies. (caddis fly)
20. I am a ferocious insect. I eat fish, tadpoles, and other small water creatures. I have large powerful jaws to attack water creatures much larger than myself. (water tiger)
21. I am a fast-moving body of water that often begins at a pond and ends at the sea. (river)
22. We are animals that eat only plants. (herbivores)
23. I have a tail and gills. Someday I will grow up to be a frog or salamander. (tadpole)
24. We are animals that eat meat. (carnivores)
25. We are related animals that lead double lives. We begin our lives with gills and later develop lungs. (amphibians)
26. I am the way living things are linked together by obtaining food. (food chain)
27. We are the organs that fish and tadpoles use to take in oxygen from the water. (gills)
28. I am the hard protective shell found on the outside of the crayfish or lobster. (exoskeleton)
29. I look much like my relative, the frog. Look closely, and you will see I have much bumpier skin. I also live farther away from the pond or river. (toad)
30. I am an insect that eats plants and small insects. You hear me chirping loudly on long summer evenings. (cricket)
31. We are simple green plants that have no stems, leaves, or flowers. We are an important food source for small herbivores. (algae)
32. I am the first stage of life for the dragonfly. I have powerful jaws that allow me to feed on small fish and tadpoles. (dragonfly nymph)

River and Pond Trivia Game *(cont.)*

(You are the dragonfly nymph.) I am a small body of water that is home to many different plants and animals. What am I? _____	(You are a pond.) Each of my thick heart-shaped leaves carries one flower and floats on the surface of the pond. . What am I? _____	(You are a water lily.) I have large, powerful wings to hover over the pond while I search for my food. What am I? _____	(You are a dragonfly.) I began my life as a tadpole. I live mostly in the water. I have four legs, no tail, and smooth skin. What am I? _____
(You are a frog.) I have a large, flat foot that I use to move slowly up and down pond plants in my search for food. What am I? _____	(You are a water snail.) I have webbed feet for swimming and a flexible neck for grabbing food underwater. My feathers are covered with an oily coating. What am I? _____	(You are a duck.) I have four webbed feet that help me swim, and I carry a hard, protective shell on my back. What am I? _____	(You are a turtle.) We are clumps of frogs' eggs that float on the surface of the pond. What are we? _____
(You are jelly babies.) I am a six-legged insect that easily walks on the water's surface. What am I? _____	(You are a water strider.) I am a relative of the frog. I, too, was once a tadpole. Now, in addition to my four legs, I also have a tail. What am I? _____	(You are a salamander.) I have a streamlined body that's great for swimming quickly. I also have three sharp spines on my back. What am I? _____	(You are a stickleback.) I look like a tiny boat rowing across the surface of the water, but I am really an insect. My back legs look like oars. What am I? _____
(You are a water boatman.) I am a small, furry mammal with a very long tail. I live along the river bank and feed mainly on plants and berries. What am I? _____	(You are a water rat.) I am related to the crab or lobster. I have a protective outer shell called an exoskeleton. What am I? _____	(You are a crayfish.) I am related to the salmon. I also swim upstream to lay my eggs. What am I? _____	(You are a trout.) I am a tiny fish, only two inches (5 cm) long. I can lay up to 2,000 eggs. What am I? _____

River and Pond Trivia Game *(cont.)*

(You are a minnow.) I have a long, smooth body that moves from side to side across the surface of the water. Some people think I look like an eel. What am I?	(You are a water snake.) I am a nocturnal mammal that flies low over the water to catch my favorite meal, insects. What am I?	(You are a bat.) My larvae hatch from eggs. I build a protective tube of sand and plant matter to protect their soft bodies. What am I?	(You are a caddis fly.) I am a ferocious insect. I eat fish, tadpoles, and other small water creatures. I have large, powerful jaws to attack water creatures much larger than myself. What am I?
(You are a water tiger.) I am a fast-moving body of water that often begins at a pond and ends at the sea. What am I?	(You are a river.) We are animals that eat only plants. What are we?	(You are herbivores.) I have a tail and gills. Someday I will grow up to be a frog or salamander. What am I?	(You are a tadpole.) We are animals that eat meat. What are we?
(You are carnivores.) We are related animals that lead double lives. We begin our lives with gills and later develop lungs. What are we?	(You are amphibians.) I am the way living things are linked together by obtaining food. What am I?	(You are the food chain.) We are the organs that fish and tadpoles use to take in oxygen from the water. What are we?	(You are gills.) I am the hard, protective shell found on the outside of the crayfish or lobster. What am I?
(You are an exoskeleton.) I look much like my relative, the frog. Look closely, and you will see I have much bumpier skin. I also live farther away from the pond or river. What am I?	(You are the toad.) I am an insect that eats plants and small insects. You can hear me chirping loudly on long summer evenings. What am I?	(You are a cricket.) We are simple green plants that have no stems, leaves, or flowers. We are an important food source for small herbivores. What are we?	(You are algae.) ★ I am the first stage of life for the dragonfly. I have powerful jaws that allow me to feed on small fish and tadpoles. What am I?

Bibliography

Nonfiction

Bailey, Jill and Jerome Bruandet. *Frogs in Three Dimensions*. Viking Penguin, 1992.

Cole, Joanna. *The Magic School Bus Hops Home: A Book About Animal Habitats*. Scholastic, Inc., 1995.

Fleming, Denise. *In the Small, Small Pond*. Henry Holt and Company, Inc., 1993.

Harlow, Rosie and Gareth Morgan. *175 Amazing Nature Experiments*, 1992.

Jennings, Terry. *The Young Scientist Investigates Pond Life*. Children's Press, 1985.

Kopp, Janie. *Frog Math: Predict, Ponder, and Play*. LHS Gems, 1992.

Lacey, Elizabeth A. *The Complete Frog: A Guide for the Very Young Naturalist*. Lothrop, Lee, and Shepard Books, 1989.

Lavies, Bianca. *Lily Pad Pond*. Penguin Books USA, Inc., 1989.

Parker, Steve. *Eyewitness Books: Pond and River*. Dorling Kindersley Limited, 1988.

Wyler, Rose. *An Outdoor Science Book: Puddles and Ponds*. Julian Messner/Simon and Schuster, Inc., 1990.

Fiction

Kellogg, Steven. *The Mysterious Tadpole*. Dial, 1979.

Poetry and Music

Felleman, Hazel. *The Best Loved Poems of the American People*. Doubleday, 1936.

Prelutsky, Jack. *The Random House Book of Poetry For Children*. Random House, 1983.

Magazines

Many educational magazines come out with wonderful articles on pond and river animals, along with excellent material for future units of study. Here are a few of the best, which you can add to your research center:

Zoobooks	**Ranger Rick**	**My Big Backyard**
P.O. Box 85384	8925 Leesburg Pike	8925 Leesburg Pike
San Diego, CA 92186	Vienna, VA 22184	Vienna, VA 22184
1-800-992-5034	1-800-588-1650	1-800-588-1650

Computer Software

Exploring the Nardoo: Multimedia CD-ROM. The Learning Team. For information call 1-800-793-Team; Fax 914-273-2227; http://learningteam.org

Answer Key

Page 9
1. Any three of the following plants: algae, duckweed, waterfern, pondweed, water milfoil, water lilies, rushes, cattails, bur reeds, marsh marigold, willows and alders.
2. The plants provide food for many of the small pond animals.

Page 23
1. fact
2. fact
3. opinion
4. fact
5. fact
6. fact
7. opinion
8. fact
9. opinion
10. fact
11. fact
12. fact
13. opinion
14. opinion
15. fact
16. fact
17. fact
18. opinion

Page 27
1. 4 centimeters
2. 1 centimeter
3. 10 centimeters
4. 7 centimeters
5. 11 centimeters
6. 3 centimeters
7. 8 centimeters
8. 5 centimeters

Page 35
1. carnivores
2. spawn
3. amphibian
4. pollution
5. compound
6. predator

7. tadpoles
8. mammals
9. herbivores

Page 38
1. 4 miles
2. 2 miles
3. 4 miles
4. 2 miles
5. 2 miles
6. Answers will vary.

Page 45
lily pad
waterfowl
dragonfly
cattail
duckweed
bluegill

Page 53
1. 11 frogs
2. 13 fireflies
3. 8 salamanders
4. 12 eggs
5. 6 mosquitoes
6. 7 minnows
7. 7 geese
8. 10 fish

Page 57
1. Freddie Frog
2. 4 feet
3. 34 feet
4. Nicky Newt
5. 3
6. 3
7. 1 foot
8. 19 feet
9. Legs are adapted for jumping.
10. Answers will vary.

Page 60
1. The daylight hours and temperature increase.
2. The pond animals grow and become more active. The plants begin to

grow.
3. Tadpoles and other small animals eat plants. They are herbivores. Small meat-eaters eat the herbivores. They are carnivores. The small carnivores then become food for the larger meat-eaters.
4. The remains of plants and animals provide food and minerals for other pond plants and animals.
5. Some pond animals lay eggs, and some fatten up in anticipation of winter. Pond plants are drying out and beginning to die.
6. It is easier to find food because it is more abundant in the spring.
7. Answers will vary.
8. Answers will vary.

Page 65
a. dorsal fin
b. adipose fin
c. lateral line
d. tail
e. pectoral fin
f. silver belly
g. ventral fin
h. anal fin